NO
SUBSTITUTE
FOR
VICTORY

NO
SUBSTITUTE
FOR
VICTORY

Frank J. Johnson

"Once war is forced upon us, there is no other alternative than to apply every available means to bring it to a swift end. War's very object is victory, not prolonged indecision."

"In war there is no substitute for victory."

General of the Army DOUGLAS MACARTHUR
Address to the United States Congress
April 19, 1951

HENRY REGNERY COMPANY
Chicago 1962

ACKNOWLEDGMENTS

In the preparation of this book I am greatly indebted to my many friends and colleagues who reviewed the manuscript. Their suggestions, criticisms and encouragement are deeply appreciated.

A special acknowledgment is due to Mr. Jameson Campaigne, whose excellent book *American Might and Soviet Myth* was a source of inspiration to speak out myself on the dangers which now face our country.

My very great thanks go also to my wife, Sally, who, in addition to being wife, mother, and critic, spent so very many long and tedious hours typing the manuscript.

Library of Congress Catalog Card Number: 62-10711
Copyright © 1962 by Henry Regnery Company
Manufactured in the United States of America

DEDICATION

To the children of America — may they continue to grow up in the land of liberty.

CONTENTS

FOREWORD

The people of the United States are concerned.

The world is in a state of turmoil.

It is evident that strife will increase in many areas of the world, Berlin, Latin America, Southeast Asia, Africa, the Middle East and even in Europe. The United States will be confronted in the immediate future with a whole series of crises, any one of which may determine whether the United States will continue to be a great nation.

Why is this?

This is because the Soviet Union is attempting to carry out her avowed aim of forty years to dominate the world. Her recent scientific successes in missiles and space, her political advances in Cuba and Asia, have served to replace the old inferiority complex with arrogance and inflated self-confidence. Our own forbearance and reluctance to take action promptly are interpreted by the Communists as loss of moral stamina and virility. Khrushchev's recent speeches and actions indicate his intention to force issues on the West at an ever increasing rate. He appears bent on testing his premise that the

Western World in general, and the United States in particular, no longer have the will to win.

This is grim competition for supremacy, for survival, in all fields and in all areas, and it will last until either the Western World or the Communists win.

The United States is the leader of the Western World. What happens to the free world is largely dependent on what the United States decides to do, and on what she does do.

We are the most powerful nation on earth. We have the greatest military power, the greatest economic power, the most brilliant scientists in the world. We have developed a system of government which has been remarkably successful in maintaining the rights of individuals and the dignity of man. We lead the world in technology. We have the highest standard of living, greater individual opportunity, more educational facilities than any other nation. We have nearly everything that other nations are striving for.

Yet the trend of events in the last few years has not been in our favor. We are not winning.

We are losing because we have not resolved to win.

This is the basic premise of this provocative book.

We may be losing because vast numbers of our people are not even conscious that the race is on, let alone the consequences of failure to win. This is why Mr. Johnson's book has a claim on the thoughtful and patriotic citizen of this country.

In strong simple language, Mr. Johnson analyzes past events, the Russian moves and United States moves and comes to the conclusion in each case that where we acted with determination and strength, Communism has been stopped. When we have displayed fear or indecision, it has advanced. What might be if the United States were to act with the bold determination to win in the cold war is projected convincingly.

In direct, clear language, he searches the future of this "Century of Conflict" and rightfully concludes that if the United States stands ready for action instead of re-action, more peoples of the world will have real peace, real freedom, and real liberty. If the United States does not implement the will to win, the world will become a police state, ruled by ruthless Communist tyrants, and mankind will have lost its freedom.

Not everybody, including me, will agree with all the points made by the author nor on the various factors he uses to determine who will win and who will lose; but everybody will agree that the United States must win this struggle for survival and that this will take "will to win" and all that that expression implies. The vital "will to win" means we must compete in every field with all the strength, all the skill, all the imagination and all the courage that our forefathers demonstrated when they formed this great nation.

The future of this country is in the hands of its citizens. The country will go where our citizens will it to go. Our future is in our hands. We can mold it in the forge of industry and strong desire. There is truly "No Substitute for Victory."

ARLEIGH BURKE

NO
SUBSTITUTE
FOR
VICTORY

I

THE UNITED STATES
AND RUSSIA

Time is running out for the United States. Supreme in its
unequaled military might, and with its material affluence
at an unprecedented level, America stands at one of the
climactic hours of world history. We are being challenged by an enemy not so strong physically as we, but
one which employs all resources—political, psychological, technological, economic, and military—with dynamic realism and relentless opportunism. If he is not
stopped, and soon, time, for us, will run out altogether.

By mutual agreement of the two contestants, foreign
policy was the central issue of the 1960 Presidential campaign. The obvious fact that the security of the United
States has steadily declined since 1945, when we held
unchallenged predominance in the world, could not be
ignored. The harsh realities of international life have at
last begun to make an impression on the American people. We are becoming aware that there is a *direct, clear*
and *present* danger to *us,* personally. Throughout the

land, there is a rising feeling of uneasiness; a feeling that something is wrong with our present policies; a feeling of impending disaster.

Disaster does impend, but only because we have not yet really understood how to fight. History is full of examples where the lean, virile challenger overthrew the society or nation which both failed to understand the true nature of the threat against it and lacked the moral stamina to take the measures necessary for its survival. The United States stands in such a position today—besieged, fighting for its life, and not yet understanding completely either the nature of the enemy or the full consequences of the challenge which he presents.

The challenger is, of course, the Communist Empire, headed by the Soviet Union. The challenged is the entire non-Communist World. The objective of the challenger is to convert the non-Communist World to a Communist one—to establish a new World Dominion. The United States, as the only power capable of frustrating that objective, is the principal obstacle to the Communist drive for world power. Its destruction or elimination as a hostile power center—its subjugation in one form or another —is the sine qua non of ultimate Communist success. If this can be achieved, the objective of world domination is achieved also. In its broader aspects, the Cold War is between the Communist Empire and the Free World. In its basic essence, however, it is a contest between the two principal protagonists—the United States and the Soviet Union.

I begin by stating the major premises of this book: The United States is at war, not at peace. We are losing, not winning the struggle for survival which the Communists have forced upon us. We are losing because we have, so far, not resolved to win. We have not resolved to win because we have not accepted the fact that we *must* win in order to continue to exist as a free nation. We *can* win if we determine that we *shall* win. In order to win, we must change our present foreign policy. We must take the offensive.

The Soviets have promoted and accepted the totality of world struggle. They are determined to destroy the influence, power and prestige of the United States throughout the world, and to do this as a prelude to control of the United States itself and establishment of a world of Communist states run from Moscow. We have so far refused to conduct the struggle on the same terms. We do not yet realize that the only way this Soviet objective can be finally thwarted is to destroy the influence, power and prestige of the Soviet Union throughout the world. Only by smashing World Communism as the instrument of Soviet imperialism can we hope to assure our own survival as a free independent country.

During the past fifteen years, we have been bemused by a new philosophy and the new philosophers of the post-war world. This philosophy stipulates that there is a substitute for victory, and its name is negotiation. Never mind that our enemies recognize no permanent obstacle on their road to eventual world conquest. In time, say the new philosophers, their ambitions will moderate as they are forced to take into account new conditions: the Parliament of Man; the diffusion of power into a plural world of newly emerging nations; the horrors of nuclear weapons; the breakdown of the monolithic Communist empire. Or, more simply, a new generation Communist bureaucracy will evolve, less dogmatic and doctrinaire than its revolutionary predecessor. These new leaders will look inward rather than outward. They will be more responsive toward the demands of their people and less concerned with the export of revolutions.

Inherent in this new philosophy has been the rejection of "power politics," or to use the classic term, "realpolitik." This term has fallen into disrepute with Americans since the days of Theodore Roosevelt when we toyed with Empire. It has never had respectability since it was so passionately denounced by Woodrow Wilson. In place of realism, we have preferred to conduct ourselves according to a set of idealistic principles. These served us well in the years when we were protected by our oceans from any direct threat to our freedom to uphold these principles. They have served us less well since those oceans evaporated as a shield from the new tyranny which has made *us* its primary target. When the unmistakable facts of Soviet ambition jarred us into awakening to our new position front and center on the stage of history, we were unfitted psychologically and ideologically to play the role so inexorably demanded of us.

We have been dragged into the world of reality partially but not yet completely. We have accepted the necessity of possessing great military power because our enemies possessed it, but we have consistently rejected the use of military power in pursuit of our national objectives except when our enemies resorted to the overt use of force. Our diplomacy has suffered accordingly. We have allowed the horrors of nuclear war to impose restriction on our own willingness to take risks, but we

4

have failed to realize that these restrictions apply twice over to our opponents. We have often allowed ourselves to be outbluffed and have acquired the reputation in some quarters of being a "paper tiger."

We accepted realistically the necessity of rebuilding European economic and military strength because we needed a strong alliance system against what was then primarily a military challenge. From there we have gone pell mell into the world of fantasy by assuming the mission—as duty, responsibility and necessity—of transforming the economic, political and social structure of the world and leading all men into Utopia. We undertake this in the name of fighting Communism. We have failed to realize that this objective, however worthy it might be if it were attainable, is not germane to the battle with Communism, except insofar as the effort to achieve it threatens to destroy our economy and thus our ability to meet the main threat to our existence.

We cling obstinately to the belief that man is not really the imperfect creature he appears to be, that if only we can find the right formula, the Brotherhood of Man will be established, and the millennium will at last be at hand. We are sure, in some manner, that "power politics" is responsible for all of mankind's troubles. We believe that if we, the most powerful nation in the world, will renounce the traditional attributes and actions of a great power and, instead, act as a shining example of the Golden Rule, then surely we will be universally loved for our selfless virtue. We will be the Moses leading mankind to the Promised Land.

As a people, we are incorrigible optimists and political adolescents. We believe anyone who holds out hope for a painless solution to our problems. With a few notable exceptions, the new philosophers have dominated our government, our educational institutions and our information media. We live in an age choking with their platitudes and tired clichés. On all sides we hear the words and slogans of the modern day appeasers: "co-existence," "modus vivendi," "accommodation," "compromise," "neutralization."

The net effect of all this is the abandonment of the will to win. Instead of summoning the people to relentless, unyielding struggle, our leaders have continuously held out the hope that somehow the threat can be averted by negotiation, that soft words and a better atmosphere will lead to a relaxation of tension and a settlement with the Soviet Union. We will not face the full meaning of the threat to our way of life. We will not fully accept the fact that we are at war. It is called "Cold War." This is really a misnomer, because our survival is no less at stake than if we were in a hot war. The enemy's ultimate goal is nothing less than total victory. He tells us so almost daily. His goal is not negotiable. He is not open to compromise, except where such "compromise" advances his cause. He is confident that he will win. He *will* win unless we drop our optimism and delusions and determine that the victory will be *ours*.

The Cold War is an extremely complex phenomenon, but its basic issue is simple. The multiple balance of power was destroyed by the two great World Wars. We face a situation once more in the world where there are only two Great Powers, in the sense that a great power in the nuclear age is a nation capable of projecting its strength on a global scale. Historically, that situation has always resulted in the destruction of one power and the ascendancy of the other. The Communists understand this. We do not. They are on the offensive, employing the ideological and economic appeals of Communism and the power image of the Soviet Union as their spearheads. Anything in the non-Communist world is fair game to be subverted and eventually swallowed up by whatever means are most appropriate and involve the least risk. There is no timetable for this policy. Defeats and setbacks are expected and are to be taken in their stride. Other opportunities are sure to follow.

With a single exception—the overthrow of the Communist regime in Guatemala in 1954—the United States has remained on the defensive in the Cold War. We have attempted to hold what we have, but we have not attempted to *counterattack*—to retake what has been lost —to advance into the enemy's territory.

The advocates of the belief that we can survive without victory, that we can negotiate with the Communists, assert that we have entered into a new era of history. Thermonuclear weapons, they say, make outright military conquest of one society by another impossible and unthinkable. Therefore, since we have the military strength to deter a Soviet military attack, it is incorrect to speak of total victory or total defeat. Neither side can defeat the other except at the price of its own destruction. Be reassured and be patient, they tell us. Russia will come around because she must. Meanwhile, we must not rock the boat. We must not press Russia too hard lest she strike out in desperation and nuclear holocaust ensue.

The fatal flaw for ourselves in this argument is obvious. It supposes that *we* shall always stand ready to accept

nuclear holocaust rather than submit. It takes no account
of the inevitable sapping of national will which results,
and in the case of the Western World now is resulting,
when a policy is followed which forbids victory. It takes
no note of the fact that once "peace" becomes the penul-
timate end of a nation or civilization and compromise and
negotiation become its means, then it becomes increasingly difficult to accept any choice which will mean the
ruin of that policy. It takes no note of the inevitable undermining of the body politic which occurs when people
are asked to make continuing sacrifice in a contest which,
from their viewpoint, can only stretch on to infinity. It
ignores, finally, the possibility that if we fail on the plane
of political and economic warfare and become isolated,
we may *not* decide to resist if the "surrender or die"
challenge finally comes. Defeats cannot forever be concealed as victories. Lack of confidence rapidly becomes
cumulative. The Achilles Heel of the United States is its
home front. The enemy is within as well as without. He
needs only the spirit of conciliation and compromise in
which to take root and prosper.

If the argument that Soviet victory is impossible is
not valid, the accompanying assertion that the United
States cannot win the Cold War is still less true, although
victory can and must necessarily take place in a somewhat different context than victory for the Communists.
A rough analogy with the present situation may be
drawn in comparing the positions of North and South in
the American Civil War. The objective of the North
(Russia) was the total subjugation of the South and the
re-establishment of the Union (establishment of a Soviet
World Empire). The objective of the South (the United

States) was not to subjugate the North but to compel it to accept the permanency of the South as an independent nation and to *co-exist peaceably* with it. Victory for the South was to be achieved by compelling the North, by force of arms, to call off its invasion. The South's policy was essentially defensive. It hoped to inflict sufficient defeats upon the North to break its will for further "aggression" and induce it to make peace.

The initial Southern victories did shake Northern confidence and in some quarters raised serious misgivings about a continuation of the war. But they could not be decisive because they were *defensive* victories. With the single exception of Lee's brief penetration into Pennsylvania, at Gettysburg (it is believed by some that a Southern victory at Gettysburg might have won the war for the South), the North itself was never invaded on a major scale. Its people were never directly confronted with the horrors of war. So long as the war was fought over the territory of the South, as a war of attrition in which the North enjoyed the advantage of manpower and industrial superiority, the ultimate issue could never be in doubt. The South's only chance of victory lay in its ability to convince the North that the objective of re-establishing the Union was not worth the consequences of further warfare. So long as the South was forced to fight on the defensive, this was impossible.

The South, of course, cannot be blamed for the type of war it chose to fight. The war was fought in a military context and the South did not have the resources to take the offensive. Here the analogy between the South and the United States ends. The United States *does* have the ability to take the offensive if we choose to do so.

We can achieve victory over the Soviet Union and win the Cold War without having to subjugate Russia militarily. We can do this by turning the tables on Russia— by confronting the Soviets with the same choice which they now purport to offer us: peaceful co-existence or the possibility of a war in which they would be destroyed. The only way to give meaning to these alternatives is by launching a counteroffensive aimed at breaking up and liberating the Communist Empire. We must destroy, not the Soviet Union itself, but the instrument of her aggression: World Communism. Today we still have this course open to us. Tomorrow we may have only the choice of surrender or total war.

We are the challenged and Russia is the challenger. Both sides essentially understand this. We are the stronger power, militarily. Russia understands this far better than does the United States. Nevertheless, the factor of nuclear weapons makes our military superiority relative rather than absolute. Russia understands that we would not deliberately attack her except as an act of desperation. (We do not admit this possibility even to ourselves.) So long as these basic facts prevail, we can win the struggle for the world without nuclear war because victory for us does not depend upon the subjugation of Russia.

Victory, for us, depends upon preventing and *eliminating* Communist control of the relative power vacuum which exists in the world between the two poles of military power. This includes those areas already under Communist domination just as much as those areas now under Communist attack. It does not matter, appreciably, whether Communist control means complete control from Moscow, so long as it means the elimination of the influence of the United States and a greater or lesser degree of hostility toward us. Every local defeat which we suffer in this contest is one more step on the road to eventual subjugation of the United States itself. Every local defeat suffered by the Soviet Union, on the other hand, represents a defeat of greater or lesser proportions in her drive for world domination, but it does not represent a step on the road towards subjugation of the Soviet Union, because this is not and should not be the United States objective. The United States objective should be to convince the Soviet Union that her goal of world domination cannot be achieved by any means short of a war in which she could not hope to avoid destruction. In short, we must convince her that her international objectives are not only impossible to attain, but that further attempts to attain them involve the most mortal risk to herself.

In a showdown, the Soviet Union will not accept nuclear war for the sake of either taking a position away from the United States or even of holding a position against a United States attack, because her own national existence does not depend upon it. *There is no compelling reason for her to commit national suicide.*

These points will be developed in subsequent chapters. They are presented now only to refute the assertions of the new philosophers that victory for either side in the world struggle is impossible. It is quite clear that it is possible for either side. It is also quite clear that the Communists are now winning.

Reporting, in January, 1961, on the Conference of eighty-one Communist Parties held in Moscow in November, 1960, Nikita Khrushchev declared, "In recent years, the initiative in the international arena has been in the hands of the Soviet Union and the socialist countries, while the imperialist states and their governments defend themselves with their backs against the wall. Their prestige and political stock have never been so low."[1]

Ordinarily, we might be tempted to dismiss this statement as nothing more than the propaganda bombast for which the Soviet dictator is famous. Scarcely more than three weeks later, however, a new American President, John F. Kennedy, delivered his first State of the Union message. In it he made the most solemn pronouncement heard by the American people since they became aware, soon after World War II, that they were in a "Cold War" with international Communism. Kennedy's words gave substance to Khrushchev's boast:

No man entering upon this office . . . could fail to be staggered upon learning . . . the harsh enormities of the trials through which we must pass in the next four years. Each day the crises multiply. Each day their solution grows more difficult. Each day we draw nearer the hour of maximum danger, as weapons spread and hostile forces grow stronger. I feel I must inform the Congress that our analyses over the last 10 days make it clear that—in each of the principle areas of crisis—the tide of events has been running out and time has not been our friend.

In a sense, these declarations by the two men who will probably dominate the world scene, barring unforeseen circumstances, for at least the next few years, set the scene for a new phase in the great drama of the Twentieth Century. Khrushchev's speech reflected his ebullient optimism and his belief that events are confirming his conviction of Communism's ultimate triumph. Kennedy's address was not one of despair; rather it was a sober acknowledgment that despite more than fifteen years of sacrifice in blood and treasure, we are losing, not winning, the battle for survival. The areas of crisis to which the President referred were the ones of the moment: a Communist–controlled Cuba threatening to spread a Marxist revolution throughout Latin America, the step-up of the Communist attack in Laos and South Vietnam, the swirling intrigues and conflicts in the Congo, aided and encouraged by Russia, and the problem of our European alliances "partially eroded by national interest." There was the warning that "the news will get worse before it is better"; the recognition that other crises are certain to come. There was also the confident assertion that the tide will turn.

As we survey our situation in the second year of the 1960's, we may ardently wish that the President's prophecy will come true—that the tide will turn. What is certain, however, is that it will not be made true by wishing. The tide *can* be turned, but only if it is done in a very literal sense—not stopped but *turned*. This will require the most sober and realistic reappraisal of our strengths and weaknesses. It will require that we purge ourselves of our misconceptions about our enemies, our allies, the United Nations, the neutrals, and the nature of the political world in which we live. It will require a searching reanalysis of our national goals. It will require a reshaping of our national policies to face the realities of our present situation.

Let us begin with a look at the past.

II

CONTAINMENT: THE BALANCE SHEET

The principal strategy which has characterized American foreign policy towards the Soviet Union in the years since World War II has been containment. This strategy, first formally enunciated by George Kennan in July, 1947, has as its philosophical basis the belief that permanent co-existence is possible between the Communist and non-Communist worlds. As originally conceived, the policy was based on confronting the Soviet Union—there was not then a Chinese Communist threat—with unyielding strength at each point at which it sought to expand. If this could be done, it was confidently expected that Soviet power would eventually be shattered by an internal convulsion, such as a struggle for power after Stalin's death, or else the Soviet state would collapse as a result of its own internal stresses. Implicit at the time of the formulation of the doctrine of containment was the belief that the objective of permanent co-existence would be achieved in a finite, relatively short period of time. No one in 1947 spoke of a prolonged, indefinite struggle which might go on for decades.

Containment evolved during the period of shock when Americans were struggling to comprehend the astounding turn of events which followed the conclusion of World War II. After June, 1941, when Hitler turned on Russia, the American people forgot everything they had ever learned about Lenin, Stalin, and the international Communist conspiracy. They forgot about the cynical Soviet invasion of Poland in 1939, the unprovoked attack on Finland in the same year, the absorption of the Baltic States—Lithuania, Latvia and Estonia—and the seizure of the Romanian province of Bessarabia in 1940. They were oblivious to the fact that Russia at no time ever renounced the official doctrines of Communism, which postulated implacable struggle with the capitalist world. They regarded the meaningless dissolution of the Comintern—the Communist International —in 1943 as an indication that Russia would settle down as a decent state and cease the export of revolution. The idealistic assumptions which governed the formation of the United Nations merely testified to the fatal misconceptions about Soviet intentions which existed among all strata of the American people and government.

As our illusions were progressively shattered in 1946 and 1947 by the vicious attacks of Soviet propaganda, the Russian proclamation of two hostile world camps, and the brutal forced communization of Eastern Europe, we were forced into an awareness that we had eliminated one enemy only to be faced with another even more sinister. This realization did not come simultaneously to all men. The reservoir of good will which the Soviets had accrued during the period of common struggle against Hitler was not easily exhausted. As late as the 1948 elections, the doctrine of the Progressive Party testified to the considerable body of opinion which still could not believe that the Communists meant business. Communist-front organizations flourished, proclaiming that it was the United States, not Russia, which was responsible for the new tensions. A substantial portion of the American public still did not regard the Soviet menace as real.

In these circumstances, our policy makers developed a policy which was fundamentally defensive. To their credit, they accepted the historical verdict that America could no longer escape its destiny. They recognized at an early date that the centers of world power had shifted to the United States and the Soviet Union. They recognized that if the Soviet drive for power, which threatened to engulf all of prostrate Europe, were to be stopped, the United States would have to stop it. We would henceforth have to be the champion of Western Civilization. Containment was a policy which represented at least some degree of realism by a government whose wartime predecessor had been almost completely blind to Soviet ambitions. It was a policy which required considerable political courage in the face of an electorate which was still thinking in terms of a return to "normalcy."

The fact nevertheless remains that containment was still only a half-way measure based on an unrealistic long-range estimate. It was a compromise between complete inaction and a resolve to come fully to grips with a threat which had existed since 1917, but which the shattering effects of World War II had made acute.

Power was concentrated almost exclusively in the hands of the United States and Russia, but the balance lay incontestably with the United States. We failed to make effective use of this circumstance.

The Cold War, up to the present, may be roughly divided into three periods. The first was 1946-49, when the battleground was primarily in Europe. However, the first direct confrontation between the United States and Russia occurred early in 1946, in the Middle East, over the continued presence of Soviet troops in the Iranian province of Azerbaijan, contrary to the provisions of the agreement which had allowed them to enter the area during the war. The first war scare arose over this crisis. The significance of this incident was, unfortunately, not fully understood. Only by the implied threat of American force was the Soviet Union, after much stalling, forced out of an area over which she had obtained physical possession. Thus Moscow, for the first time, acknowledged her unwillingness to risk war with the United States in pursuit of her objectives. The Azerbaijan affair was an isolated incident unrelated to a specific strategy. A year later, containment was being formulated, but this strategy, unfortunately, did not include the idea of forcing the Communists out of any area over which they already had possession.

United States intervention, under the Truman Doctrine, prevented the Communist takeover of Greece and eased pressure on Turkey, but Russia won control over Eastern Europe. This was accomplished by the now classic Communist method of political infiltration into all levels of society, the formation of a coalition government and the eventual forcible elimination of all non-Communist elements. In Bulgaria, Romania, Hungary and Poland, it was done with the heavy-handed assistance of the occupying Soviet armies. Contrary to the Yalta agreement, no genuinely free elections were ever held in these nations. In Czechoslovakia, it was accomplished by a Communist coup d'état in 1948, backed up by the threat of Russian invasion. The Soviet Zone of Germany was made into a Soviet preserve. Its satellization was completed in 1949, when an East German Government was established.

In June of 1947, the first of the Foreign Aid programs was announced by Secretary of State George Marshall. Known as the Marshall Plan, this economic help was initially offered to the states of Eastern as well as Western Europe. Poland and Czechoslovakia first accepted. They had not checked with Moscow, and they were subsequently forced to change their minds. The Marshall Plan was successful in that it unquestionably aided the economic recovery of Western Europe. There was no lack of skilled labor and industrial know-how. There was not the problem of starting from scratch in an alien culture which has plagued our subsequent aid programs. It was a problem, rather, of putting a temporarily dislocated economy on its feet.

The role played by the Marshall Plan in preventing Communist subversion of Western Europe, however, is very much exaggerated. Communist effectiveness declined from its peak in France and Italy in 1947, *before* Marshall Plan aid had begun to take effect. Violent strikes and riots against the legal governments had taken on the character of insurrections. For a time, it had appeared that the Communists might seize power. They failed, essentially because they lacked broad popular support for a revolution from below, and because there was no Soviet Army to immobilize opposition to a seizure of power by a coup at the top. The Communists lacked control of the all-important ministries of the interior which controlled the police. When faced by determined opposition in areas beyond the reach of the Soviet armies, the Communists were unable to prevail. Nevertheless, they were able to establish themselves as potent political forces in France and Italy. The economic success of the Marshall Plan has done little to diminish the political strength of the Communists in those countries.

The climax of the initial Soviet drive in Europe came with the Berlin blockade in the summer of 1948. The United States resisted; we chose to checkmate the Soviet effort, and we began the Berlin airlift—although it was by no means initially clear that the airlift could do the job. Diplomatic efforts to get the Soviets to lift the blockade failed until the airlift had become an indisputable success. The possibility of war at this time was again rather freely predicted. However, neither side wished a showdown. The Western Powers did not enforce their rights to ground access to Berlin; the Soviets did not try to interfere with the airlift. The raising of the blockade in 1949 temporarily ended the Soviet drive in Europe.

There is no doubt that United States policy suffered from excessive caution during this critical period. It is true that Soviet troops, poised on the Elbe, held Western Europe as a potential hostage following the abrupt withdrawal from Europe of the great majority of American troops immediately after the war. The power position of the United States, however, was vastly superior to that of Russia. We had emerged with our homeland unscathed by war and at the peak of our strength. We had the atomic bomb; Russia did not. Her losses in men had been enormous; ours had been relatively light. The Soviet economy was in a shambles; Western Russia, a wasteland. If the thought of another war so soon after World War II was repugnant to us, it was for more so to Stalin. The Soviet people had fought bravely, although not without considerable defections, in defense of their country. But could Stalin have then driven them into a war of aggression outside the territory of Russia? Not without serious risk of rebellion at home.

There was no need, from a purely power standpoint, to acquiesce to any of the Soviet actions in Europe in 1946-49. If we had been willing to threaten war, we could have forced the Soviets to give up their hold on Eastern Europe and to allow at least genuinely neutral regimes to be established. We could, and should, have enforced our rights completely in Berlin in 1948 by employing force to reopen the land corridor. The danger of a Russian drive to the Channel was in reality non-existent. Soviet pressures eased in Europe even before American determination to halt further advances was formalized, in 1949, by the formation of the North Atlantic Treaty Organization. NATO was a military alliance formed against the threat of an overt attack against Western Europe. Although the psychological effect on Soviet policy was profound, it contributed almost nothing in its first years as a military deterrent to Soviet attack. That deterrent lay exclusively in the fact that the Soviet

Union was not prepared to involve herself in a war with the United States, still the sole possessor of both the atomic bomb and a means of delivery. The massive Soviet armies in Europe provided a false picture of Soviet strength. Containment undoubtedly prevented even further Soviet successes, but it fell short of the counteroffensive which was needed to regain promptly what had already been lost. The worst part of it was that, by taking an unrealistically optimistic view of the further development of Soviet power, we committed ourselves permanently to the defensive.

The next broad period of the Cold War is encompassed approximately by the years 1949-1956. The geographical center of the struggle shifted to the Far East. The Communists had been on the march in China and in the various insurrectionary movements in Southeast Asia since the end of World War II, but the situation did not become acute until after the fall of China. Misguided and unrealistic efforts by the United States to effect a compromise in the Chinese Civil War consistently worked to the advantage of the Communists, who utilized every truce to improve their position vis-à-vis the Nationalists under Chiang Kai-Shek. Propaganda portraying the Communists as crusading agrarian reformers and Chiang as evil and corrupt obscured the fact that the balance of power was being profoundly altered in the Far East to the disadvantage of the United States. When the Nationalist armies collapsed in 1949, there was a general feeling of good riddance among Americans. Certainly there was never any disposition by the United States to intervene with troops to halt the Communist advance in China. A year later the consequences of the loss of China were brutally brought home by the Korean War. This action merits some discussion.

Attacking initially under the false assumption that the Americans would not defend Korea, the Communists were encouraged to continue the war when it became obvious that the United States, prodded by the United Nations, would keep the war limited to the Korean peninsula. The collapse of the North Korean armies in September, 1950, prompted the United States, on the urging of General MacArthur, to attempt to administer a decisive rebuff to Communism by driving the Communists out of North Korea. Russia and China understandably wished to salvage something from the Korean misadventure if it could be done within the limits of acceptable risk. The pressures brought to bear on Washington to keep the war limited gave them this opportunity.

As MacArthur's forces advanced northward toward the Yalu River in October, 1950, Chinese forces began to cross into Korea, after the Chinese had given repeated warnings that they would intervene. They were backed up by a Mutual Assistance Treaty between Russia and China, which strongly implied, but did not specifically state, that Russia would come to China's aid if attacked.[1] The initial skirmishes with Chinese "volunteers" occurred in late October. By early November, MacArthur announced officially that the Chinese had entered the war. Despite his announcement, the United States Government refused to face up to the new situation and sought to pretend that the Chinese were not even there. MacArthur's request to bomb the Yalu bridges was denied. He began his ill-fated "home by Christmas" offensive in the hope that it might bluff the Chinese into withdrawing, or at least force them to show their hand. The Chinese and Soviets both gauged correctly that Chinese intervention in force would not bring about an expansion of the war. This was evident from the failure of the United States to act decisively at the time of the first skirmishes with the Chinese. The risk of all-out intervention was therefore an acceptable one. In early December, the massive Chinese attacks overwhelmed and split the Eighth Army and Tenth Corps and forced them to retreat from North Korea.

As it happened, Chinese intervention was not as decisive as it was thought in those bleak days of December, 1950. As the Chinese advanced southward from their Manchurian sanctuary, their logistics lines in Korea came under heavy air attack. They were unable to sustain offensives for more than a few days. MacArthur was able to stabilize his lines and then begin a counteroffensive. What seems apparent from the reports of that time, however, is that the United States was prepared to write off Korea and accept crushing defeat rather than expand the war beyond Korea. Events on the field of battle saved us from that dismal course.

In April, 1951, relations between General MacArthur and President Truman, never good, reached an impasse, and MacArthur was dismissed from his command. The issue was whether another try for complete victory should be made. MacArthur now felt he had the measure of the Chinese and that, if given a free hand to bomb their Manchurian bases, he could inflict a decisive defeat on them. President Truman and, apparently, the Joint Chiefs of Staff disagreed.[2] Uppermost in their minds was the possibility of Soviet intervention and World War III if Chinese territory were directly attacked. Our United Nations allies were also dead set against such a move. Permission was granted to conduct a military pursuit of the Chinese armies across the 38th parallel, but this time there was to be no attempt at complete occupation of all of Korea. The Chinese armies, in fact, began to fall back in the late spring of 1951. They might well have been dealt a crushing defeat. However, they asked for peace talks, and the United States complied.[3] There then followed two long bloody years of positional warfare while the Communists stalled and built up an impregnable defense line. The opportunity for victory slipped through our fingers.

The Korean War is significant for a number of reasons: First, it reaffirmed the doctrine of containment and promoted the fatal belief that there *is* a substitute for victory. Second, we made a false estimate of Soviet military power and an unrealistic assessment of Soviet willingness to fight the United States which continues to this day. Third, we failed to seize the opportunity to discredit, and possibly bring down, the Chinese Communists by destroying the cream of their armies in Korea. In fact, we boosted Communist China's prestige by allowing her to boast that she had successfully met America on the field of battle. Fourth, by accepting less than our goal of a reunited Korea, we suffered a loss of face in Asia. Fifth, we began the policy of allowing our Allies and the United Nations to exert undue influence on American policy.

To his staff, General MacArthur said of the Korean War: "The overriding deficiency incident to the conduct of the War in Korea by the United Nations lies in its lack of will for victory. Underlying the whole problem has always been the indeterminate question as to whether or not the Soviet contemplates the conquest of the World by military means rather than by those of more peaceful persuasion.

"If it intends to use force, the time and place will be at its own initiative and could not fail to be influenced by the fact that in the atomic area, the lead of the United States is being steadily diminished with the passage of time. So likewise is the great industrial potential of the United States as compared with the Communist World.

"In short, it has always been my own belief that any action we might take to resolve the Korean problem could not in itself be a controlling factor in the precipitation of a world conflict."[4]

Following the termination of the Korean War in July, 1953, the position of the French in Indo-China rapidly deteriorated. Since attempting to regain control over their colony in 1946, following the Japanese occupation, the French had become involved in an increasingly bitter struggle with the Communist Viet Minh guerillas. After the Chinese Communist conquest of China, the common border with Indo-China allowed the Chinese to funnel aid across the frontier to the Viet Minh, who gradually drove the French from the border areas. By the winter of 1953–1954, the French position was critical. The Viet Minh controlled the countryside in the northern portion of Vietnam, around Hanoi, and were infiltrating into Laos, Cambodia, and Southern Vietnam. The French decided to stake all on the defense of the great fortress of Dien Bien Phu, in North Vietnam, near the border of Laos. At the same time, they prodded the United States to intervene on their behalf.

As the Indo-China crisis mounted and the United States contemplated the pros and cons of intervention, it was obvious that another Korea-type conflict loomed if the Chinese should once more send in "volunteers" in large numbers. Secretary of State Dulles, therefore, enunciated in January, 1954, a new American policy, known as "massive retaliation." This policy seemed to rule out another limited war. Dulles declared that henceforth the United States would retaliate massively "at places and times of our own choosing" against any aggressor which might launch an armed attack against Free World territory.

With this implicit warning to the Chinese to stay out of Indo-China, Dulles began his policy of "brinkmanship." As the Communist noose tightened around Dien Bien Phu, Vice President Nixon talked openly of sending American troops if the French collapsed. It was enough to cause the Communists to enter into an international conference to discuss an Indo-China settlement. This conference met at Geneva in late April, but the Viet Minh persisted in the siege of Dien Bien Phu. It became apparent that only direct American aid could save the beleagured garrison. After much indecision, we declined to commit our forces in Indo-China and Dien Bien Phu fell in May, 1954. The French position was now desperate, and a total collapse threatened throughout Indo-China.

The Viet Minh held the military advantage after the fall of Dien Bien Phu, but the United States threat of intervention, backed up by the new policy of "massive retaliation" was not without its effect in Moscow and Peking. They decided to settle for what they already had rather than press for a conquest of all Indo-China. The result was the Geneva settlement of July, 1954, in which the Communists took possession of North Vietnam. Laos and Cambodia, the other Indo-China states, became independent. The United States did not sign the accord and withheld its blessing; privately, however, it was regarded as the best to be hoped for under the circumstances. For France it was the virtual end of her influence in Indo-China. Her position was gradually taken over by the United States. This compounded French resentment at our failure to come to the aid of Dien Bien Phu and left a legacy of bitterness in France which was reflected, seven years later, when Indo-China once again occupied the world spotlight.

The Indo-China settlement marked a temporary end to the Communist military offensive in Asia. The lines between the two contending forces were now hardening. The United States was building up a series of alliance systems committing us to the defense of the areas around the Sino-Soviet periphery. Following the Geneva agreement, the Southeast Asia Treaty Organization was created to provide for a common defense against further Communist aggression in that area. In the Middle East, the Baghdad Pact, between Britain, Turkey, Iraq, Iran, and Pakistan, was set up in 1955. The United States, though not a member, underwrote it as a defense against any Soviet push into the Middle East. In Europe, NATO continued to evolve through the tribulations of trying to provide some measure of German rearmament, the only course which offered any hope of blunting a Soviet ground offensive. The European Defense Community, which would have provided for a common European army, foundered on French opposition in 1954, but West Germany was admitted to NATO in 1955 and began a slow build up of her forces.

None of these alliance systems offered in themselves any deterrent to overt Communist attack. They were in no case alliances among equals, for military power rested almost exclusively with the United States. The Communists were given pause by the fact that armed incursion into any of these areas risked war with the United States and the knowledge that this war *would probably not remain limited* under the doctrine of "massive retaliation." Despite the completely unbalanced power relationship, the United States granted political equality to at least its major allies, Britain and France. American policy became increasingly entangled in the alliances which we created. In taking on world-wide commitments, we began to deliver our freedom of action into the hands of those whom we undertook to defend.

At the time of the fall of Dien Bien Phu, the United States chalked up its one success to date in expelling the Communists from an area in which they had established themselves. This was Guatemala. A pro-Communist regime under President Arbenz was expelled by an outside force of Guatemalan exiles with the clandestine assistance of the United States. Four years later a much more serious threat was to erupt under the banner of Fidel Castro. This time clandestine assistance would not be enough.

Another extremely important development of the early 1950's was the tremendous increase in the destructive-

28

ness of warfare. The development of the hydrogen bomb created the spectre of civilization itself perishing in the flames of nuclear war. A technological revolution brought about the era of missile warfare, when not only the nuclear weapon but its means of delivery became all important. As we shall see later in this book, these factors, aided by the death of Stalin in 1953, had a profound effect on the Soviet strategy for world conquest. The power balance continued to be overwhelmingly in favor of the United States, since our growing network of overseas bases and our Strategic Air Command gave us a means of delivering nuclear weapons to Russia which the Soviets could not match. The ability to destroy Russia completely lay in the hands of the United States with no corresponding Russian capability.

The circumstances were never better for launching a counteroffensive. However, the fear of nuclear weapons and the continuing exaggeration of the Soviet's own military strength combined to induce us to throw away our advantages. We also thought that containment was finally paying off. Stalin's death created the problem of succession foreseen by Kennan six years earlier. The execution of Beria, and the ousting of Malenkov as Premier in January, 1955, afforded reason to believe that Russia might be torn apart by a power struggle. A "peace offensive" emanated from Moscow. The Big Four heads of government met at Geneva in 1955 in a spirit of considerable harmony. The "agreements" reached suggested a settlement of the German question might be achieved and created the "Spirit of Geneva." It was the apex of hopes for a peaceful settlement of the Cold War. The United States was neatly maneuvered out of taking any advantage of its superior power until Soviet scientists could create a counterdeterrent to "massive retaliation."

The finale of the second period of the Cold War took place in the streets of Budapest in October–November, 1956. During the presidential campaign of 1952, John Foster Dulles had promised that the Republicans, if elected, would work for the liberation of Eastern Europe. He seemed to promise a policy of rolling back the Soviet Empire. The first opportunity to put this policy into effect came in June, 1953, when there were serious anti-Communist riots in East Berlin. These were quickly put down, however, and there was little of a concrete nature that the United States could do. The Hungarian Revolt, on the other hand, posed a direct challenge to the policy of liberation, which had never officially been retracted. (The issue of Eastern Europe was raised at the Geneva Summit meeting, although it was promptly dropped after Khrushchev's scornful rejection of any discussion.) The Voice of America and Radio Free Europe had done nothing to discourage a rising. Now it came and it was crushed in blood while the United States did nothing but engage in futile denunciations of the Soviet action in the United Nations. By its inaction, the United States served formal notice that the Communist sphere was inviolate. We announced, in effect, that we would play the game on Communist terms. The battleground would be limited to the Free World. "Liberation" as a policy died with Hungary.

However, we did not understand the implications of Hungary, nor its tremendous significance as a turning point in the Cold War. Had we been willing to make use of our still incomparable nuclear superiority over Russia and take a calculated risk by intervening in Hungary, there was an excellent chance that the Cold War could have been decisively swung in our favor by means of a breakup of Communist control over Eastern Europe. Certainly there was never a better moral issue on which to stake a showdown with the Soviet Union. This was our great opportunity and we failed. We were not willing to risk a naked power confrontation with Russia when we held the superior cards. By failing to do so, we began to give substance to the false Soviet claims that we no longer had the military advantage. The stalemate began to break down in Russia's favor.

Of course there are many reasons given for our failure to act in Hungary: the Atlantic Alliance was shattered by the unfolding events at Suez and was in no position or frame of mind to take concerted action in Hungary; public opinion would not have supported the risk of nuclear war over Hungary; events in any case moved too fast for effective intervention. The "logic" of these excuses for inaction is not likely to save us from the judgment of history. We possessed the capability to act unilaterally. Had we been willing to send even a battalion of troops to Hungary, particularly in the days before the Soviets intervened, we would have forced on Russia the decision of whether to risk war by a direct clash with American forces. Instead, the United States was weighed in the balance and found wanting. The will to action was lacking. The Soviets suffered a temporary propaganda set-back in Hungary but won a strategic victory, since the Eastern European dream of liberation was crushed in bitter disillusion. The people there are now much more prone to accept their fate. Russia has thereby been able to relax her grip on this area and permit a somewhat greater degree of freedom. This increased stability has contributed to the Soviet effort to create the image of a new U. S. S. R., less harsh and dictatorial than under Stalin. The bloody repression of Hungary's bid for freedom is all too easily forgotten by the non-Communist World, but American inaction will never be forgotten by those who believed that our goal was truly their liberation.

The 1949–1956 period may be broadly categorized as a period of transition between the unabashed efforts of Stalin to grab everything he could by force and the more subtle but infinitely more dangerous advance of Communist influence under Khrushchev. The military threat predominated in the thinking of American strategists; but the extent of military superiority of the United States over the Soviet Union was never fully appreciated, and no attempt was made to capitalize on it. We still thought in terms of the dangers of an all-out Soviet attack, whereas such an action was, from the point of view of the Soviets, unthinkable. During this period, the United States took on global commitments of an economic and military character, but we became frozen into a defensive posture which completely surrendered the initiative to the Communists. The two great opportunities to deliver crushing defeats to our enemies, when the moral right was indisputably on our side, were allowed to pass—in Korea in 1951 and Hungary in 1956. We still thought in terms of the original theories of containment—that Russia would be rent by internal pressures and that permanent coexistence was a realistic prospect. We were thus unprepared to confront the new Communist offensive which has, in the space of five years, rendered our alliances virtually impotent and brought the sense of deep foreboding to the American people and the rising crescendo of exultation from Moscow.

This most recent period of the Cold War dates from about 1956 to at least the end of the Eisenhower Administration. It followed the resolution of the problem of Stalin's successor in favor of Nikita Khrushchev and the development of an entirely new Soviet strategy. This strategy abandoned the idea of overt military attack in favor of the indirect approach. The challenge is ambiguous rather than direct. It offers us no clear-cut issue on which to make a stand. It has been featured by Russia's efforts to promote neutralism generally, and among America's allies in particular, and to increase her influence among the great number of newly emerging uncommitted or "neutral" states. The major Soviet objective has been to create the impression that the balance of power has shifted to the Soviet Union and thus effect the political neutralization of American military power as a deterrent to further Communist expansion. If this objective is achieved, the Soviets confidently expect that the realization of a Communist world will follow rather quickly.

The Communists have made a great deal of progress toward their goal. As early as 1955, their conclusion of an arms deal with Egypt began their new policy of cultivating and penetrating neutral nations. During the ensuing build-up of tension in the Middle East, the Soviets shrewdly added fuel to the flames by appearing as the champions of Arab nationalism. The Suez affair in 1956, which was a direct outgrowth of Soviet fishing in these troubled waters, gave the Russians their first opportunity to impress the world with their new military might. Britain and France were compelled to withdraw from their Suez action by a combination of American pressure and violent British Labor opposition (not, it must be emphasized, by the United Nations). The Soviets attempted to seize credit for the withdrawal by threatening to rain rockets on Britain and France unless they got out. The threat was a bluff, but it electrified the world. The military balance of power, so long held by the West, now seemed to be shifting.

The following year, in 1957, the Soviets were able to announce the double feat of launching an ICBM and the first Sputnik. These appeared to be indisputable examples of Soviet technological superiority over the United States. The alleged threat of a Turkish attack on left-leaning Syria in the fall of 1957 gave the Soviets another opportunity to threaten use of their rockets. From then on, Russian propagandists have repeatedly stressed the theme of growing Soviet military might and have attempted to portray the United States as increasingly deterred from launching a war by the fear of devastating Soviet retaliation.

Side by side with the image of an all-powerful Soviet Union, the Soviets have zealously cultivated the image of a peace-loving, benevolent Russia intent only on demonstrating the superiority of Communism over Capitalism as an economic system. Their slogan is "peaceful co-existence." Their goal is to outstrip the United States in production. They wish to prove to the industrially underdeveloped nations that their system and their ideology offer the way toward progress. It is a double-barrelled approach. The Communists assert they will win because they are becoming stronger than the West. But this is nothing to dread, they say; the Soviet Union is living proof that this triumph of Communism will be of benefit to mankind.

In this stage of their new offensive, the Soviets have not as yet sought to effect actual Communist takeovers in the uncommitted areas. There is, in fact, evidence that Khrushchev ordered the Communist Party in Iraq to go slow on any bid for outright power following the nationalist coup against the pro-Western government in 1958, which took Iraq out of the Baghdad Pact. *The important thing, from Khrushchev's standpoint, was that Iraq was removed from the United States column.* For the time being, any left-leaning neutral, whose officials and people are genuinely impressed with the Soviet success story and who can be counted on to oppose any resolute United States anti-Communist policy, is a more effective tool of Soviet policy than an outright Communist state.

During this period, the United States has attempted to meet the new Soviet challenge primarily through the device of foreign aid in ever greater amounts. This policy has generally been a failure. It has enabled many of the neutrals to practice blackmail by threatening to grant advantages or concessions to the Soviets if we do not meet their demands. It has produced justifiable pique among some of our most loyal allies, who wonder why a neutral should receive more assistance than a staunch friend. Regardless of whether or not economic assistance has contributed in any substantial measure to improvement of the recipients' economies, it has not been the *decisive* factor in influencing the political orientation of a single foreign government: we have scrupulously avoided attaching any such condition to our aid. The political make-up of the world is tending increasingly to revolve around the power balance between East and West, and specifically between the United States and the Soviet Union. It is here that the United States has *appeared* to be falling behind during the last five years. No amount of foreign aid can redress this situation.

The United States position has eroded before the Soviet advance largely because we have failed to act in a decisive manner. As the Communists have gradually stepped up their pressures and intrigues, we have re-acted in a way which has given substance to Soviet claims of military and technological superiority.

Following the Iraq coup in July, 1958, we would not allow Turkey to take military action to restore the situation on the grounds that this would be aggressive and might provoke Soviet retaliation. The Soviets were able to claim that it was they who saved Iraq from Western attack. Our intervention in Lebanon, while justified and correct under the circumstances, was no victory over Communism and involved no risk. Russia was not involved in Lebanon. Her prestige was not at stake and did not suffer.

The strong American reaction to the Chinese probing action at Quemoy in the fall of 1958 definitely deterred an attack on the islands, but the Chinese Communists were allowed to save face, and the lesson of their back-down in the face of American force was largely lost. Instead, they got credit for a willingness to be reasonable while we began to look about for some way to disentangle ourselves from the defense of the Offshore Islands.

Khrushchev's original bluff of the six months' ultimatum on Berlin in 1958 was called, but in a manner which seemed to leave the door open for a gradual retreat at the conference table.

The communization of Cuba was allowed to proceed without American counteraction because, it was said, we did not wish to provoke Latin American public opinion. However, the Vice President of the United States also argued, during the 1960 presidential election campaign, that aid to the Cuban revolutionaries might provoke Soviet intervention in a Cuban civil war.[5]

In 1960, the United States reacted indecisively to the anti-American coup in Laos and later made no effort to deter Soviet intervention in the civil war. In the vain belief that the country could be neutralized we reversed our efforts to maintain it as pro-American. Always we profess our fear that strong action might provoke war.

The Soviet achievements in space, which have been so dramatized since 1957, are not in themselves serious threats to United States military superiority over the Soviet Union. The Soviets have been allowed to exploit them as such, however, because at no time have we ever given the world a positive demonstration that the Soviets are bluffing. We have never forced the Communists to back down in such a way that we could claim a clear-cut victory. We have never defeated them in a *power* sense. Instead, by our apparent weakness in foreign policy, we are confirming the Soviet pretense of military superiority. We consistently strive to avoid placing the Soviet

37

Union in a position where her prestige is at stake, fearing to provoke her into rash action. We do not know that she cannot be provoked unless it suits her purpose. The Soviets, on the other hand, seek above all else to damage American prestige in any way that they can. When they win a victory, their propagandists make sure the world knows that the power of the United States has been further weakened.

Like a broken record, the United States drones on and on that its objective is to maintain "peace" and extend "freedom" throughout the world. We have not extended freedom anywhere, and the Soviets have pre-empted both words, "peace" and "freedom," for their own purposes—just as they have appropriated our other favorite word, "democracy." All too often, our use of the word "peace" smacks of appeasement.

The President's Commission on National Goals issued the report, "Goals for Americans," in 1960. On foreign policy it declared:

The basic foreign policy of the United States should be the preservation of its own independence and free institutions. Our position before the world should be neither defensive nor belligerent. We should cooperate with nations whose ideals and interests are in harmony with ours. We should seek to mitigate tensions and search for acceptable areas of accommodation with opponents. The safeguarded reduction of armaments is an essential goal.

We must stand firm wherever, as in Berlin, our commitments and interests are squarely opposed to those of the Soviets. At whatever cost we must maintain strategic and tactical forces of sufficient strength to deter the

Communist powers from surprise attack and to cope with military aggression even on a limited scale.

In nations subject to Communist domination or influence, our hope must be that the right of self-determination will ultimately be achieved.[6]

There are many fine expressions in those passages, but nowhere do we say that our goal is the *defeat of Communism*. We speak, for example, of deterrence to overt Communist military attack. We say we must stand firm where our commitments and interests are "squarely" opposed to those of the Soviets. We say nothing about cases where the challenge is indirect and the issues not so clear-cut. Where we have no firm commitment or where the clash of interests is not plain and direct, retreat is apparently permissible. Referring to the nations under Communist dominance, we merely express the "hope" that they will someday achieve the right of self-determination. Independence and world freedom are our objectives, but we must try to achieve them without victory.

General David Sarnoff, writing for the *Life* series on National Goals in 1960 observed: "Survival of the free world—side by side with an unfree world—has been and remains the maximum goal of Western diplomacy. Not the weakening and eventual defeat of Communism but a lasting accommodation seems to mark the farthest reach of hope. It is scarcely a vision to inspire confidence or zeal, and in any case it is utterly utopian, because two parties are needed to make an accommodation."[7]

Summing up our over-all national strategy, it might be described as "hopeful co-existence" where our objective is essentially "peace" at any reasonable price. The failure

39

of American policy so far has been due in large measure to the unwillingness of the American people and their government to take risks to assure the survival of the United States. Communist power has enlarged in relation to our own because we have been unwilling decisively to check that enlargement. We have always possessed the power to do it at any time we chose. Our problem has never been a lack of effective military strength, but rather a philosophy which deprives us of the will to use it. We could have prevented the Communist takeover of Eastern Europe; we could have prevented the fall of China; we could have inflicted a decisive defeat on Communism in Korea; we could have prevented the loss of North Vietnam; we could have assured the success of the Hungarian Revolution; we could have prevented the loss of Laos. But we could not do those things with words; we could have done them with force. That we did not is the measure of our weakness and our blindness.

The foremost goal of the Eisenhower Administration was to avoid war. Mr. Eisenhower expressed it in his final State of the Union Message: "The continuing goal is peace, liberty and well being—for others as well as ourselves"; and in his Farewell Address to the nation: "Happily I can say that war has been avoided. Steady progress toward our ultimate goal has been made." Unfortunately, far more progress has been made in recent years towards the Communist goal than toward our own.

The words of the Communist Manifesto, issued in December, 1960, to summarize the Moscow meeting of Communist Parties, which had just ended, are chilling because they are partly true:

The chief result of these (last three) years is the rapid growth of the might and international influence of the world socialist system, the vigorous process of disintegration of the colonial system under the impact of the national liberation movement, the intensification of class struggles in the capitalist world, and the continued decline and decay of the world capitalist system; the superiority of the forces of socialism over those of imperialism, of the forces of peace over those of war, is becoming ever more marked in the world arena.[8]

In echo of those words, the Soviets scored yet another "first" by placing a man in orbit around the earth in April, 1961. As Yuri Gagarin stood with Khrushchev in triumph atop the Lenin mausoleum in Red Square, he shouted, "Long live our Socialist Motherland!" Back thundered the approval of hundreds of thousands of ecstatic Russians. Khrushchev did not fail also to make military propaganda; he used the occasion to declare that the space feat had given Soviet defenses a "colossal superiority over the West." Unfortunately, much of the world believes his boast.

This is the Russia which confronts us in the nuclear age. The belief so cherished during the past fifteen years that the Soviet regime would some day seek a genuine accommodation with the West was never so bankrupt, and yet many people still seem to be convinced that we can negotiate our differences. They still nurture the vain hope that if we can just stand off the Communists a little longer—ten years is frequently mentioned—things will get better.

They will not get better. As Philip Mosely, in a recent issue of *Foreign Affairs* concludes, "The Soviet system will grow in economic, military and scientific strength during the 1960's." These strengths "will enable its leaders to devote greater rather than smaller resources . . . to achieving the world-wide purposes that have been proclaimed in an evolving pattern of interpretation by Lenin and Stalin and now by Khrushchev."[9]

President Kennedy in his Inaugural Address offered to negotiate with the Communists: "So let us begin anew —remembering on both sides that civility is not a sign of weakness, and sincerity is always subject to proof. Let both sides explore what problems unite us instead of belaboring those problems which divide us." These words must have produced some cynical laughter in the Kremlin. Shortly afterward, the American Ambassador to the Soviet Union, Llewelyn Thompson, was allowed to cool his heels for over one week in Moscow until Khrushchev deigned to allow him to fly to Siberia to present the President's views on Laos and other issues. Subsequently, demand after demand for a cease fire in Laos went unanswered or was evaded while the Soviet airlift of supplies to the Communist Pathet Lao continued. Laos, we said, was to be the "test" of Soviet sincerity and willingness to negotiate. This whole sorry spectacle of American indecision and retreat in Southeast Asia was an excellent example of what happens in negotiation when the Communists are holding the high cards.

The still prevalent idea that the U. S. S. R. can be "persuaded" to abandon its drive for world conquest is totally absurd. The Soviet leaders are confirmed in all their expectations about Communism's inevitable triumph. And why not? They have not suffered a single major defeat which would cause them to doubt their ultimate victory.

In the year, 1961, there is every indication that a new

and more deadly phase in the Cold War is beginning. We stand in the worst position which we have occupied in the struggle with Communism since World War II. The trend in the world is for one country after another to switch from support of United States policies to a so-called neutrality, which more often than not favors the Soviet Union. Neutrality stems in part from the cynical belief of some countries that there is more to be gained by not being too closely associated with the United States. It stems in part from fear of riding a losing horse.

The prestige of the United States is falling where it counts most; not with the Communist-agitated street mobs who riot at the slightest indication of American resistance to Communist expansion, or among the fuzzy-minded "intellectuals" to whom there is no basic difference between the United States and Russia, but among those who follow the practical school of "realpolitik." Some are our friends who are becoming dismayed at our inaction. Others are those on the sidelines who are trying to figure out who will end up as the winner. The record of United States policy in recent years is not such as to assure these people that we will survive the Communist challenge. Repeatedly, our actions seem to give an appearance of Soviet strength and American weakness. Carlos Romulo, the Philippine Ambassador to the United States, and one of our staunchest and most sincere friends, surveyed our policy and was compelled to write, almost in despair, "America, Wake Up! Shake off the course of inaction that is giving the forces of evil the right of way in this world! Face up to the blunt fact that you are now engaged in a real war and that it must be fought *and won*. This is the only alternative to defeat by default!"[10]

For a brief period, there were some indications that the United States might be waking up. The first effort to overthrow the Castro regime in Cuba by aiding the Cuban revolutionaries ended in abysmal failure because of United States unwillingness to provide military support. In the soul-searching aftermath of this fiasco, an apparently much wiser President Kennedy addressed the American Society of Newspaper Editors on April 20, 1961:

Should it ever appear that the inter-American doctrine of non-interference merely conceals or excuses a policy of non-action—if the nations of this hemisphere should fail to meet their commitments against outside Communist penetration—then I want it clearly understood that this Government will not hesitate in meeting its primary obligations which are to the security of our Nation.

The evidence is clear, and the hour is late. We and our friends will have to face the fact that we cannot postpone any longer the real issue of survival itself.

It was evident from the speech that the President had more than just Cuba in mind:

We intend to profit from this lesson. We intend to re-examine and re-orient our forces, our tactics and our institutions. We intend to intensify our efforts for a struggle in many ways more difficult than war.

For I am convinced that we possess all the necessary resources, and all the skill, and all the added strength that comes from belief in the freedom of man.

*And I am equally convinced that history will record the fact that this bitter struggle reached its climax in the late 1950's and early 1960's.**

* Italics added.

44

Unfortunately, the hope implicit in these words for a new departure in our foreign policy has not yet been realized. Castro remains, more arrogant than ever. No hand is raised against him. Everywhere we remain on the defensive; the pressures on us mount steadily; the crises come with ever greater frequency. The hour is desperately late. The struggle is indeed approaching its climax; but we still look in vain for any real sign that the outcome will be in our favor. If future historians are not to conclude that the 1960's were the last years of Western Civilization, then deeds as well as words are needed. This is a time for decisiveness and above all for boldness. Is it a time for negotiation? Consider the words of Dr. Frederick Schwarz: "To negotiate *true peace** with people who are utterly dedicated to the concept of the historical inevitability of class war and their victory is impossible. To think that we can do it is to indicate a failure to understand Communism so completely that it approaches mental illness. To the Communist, every negotiation is an act of war. Every delegation is an act of war. Every peace petition is an act of war. Every disarmament conference is an act of war."[11]

* Italics added.

III

BLUEPRINT FOR CONQUEST

To fight and conquer in all your battles is not supreme excellence; supreme excellence consists in breaking through the enemy's resistance without fighting.

Sun Tsu, 500 B.C.

The Communists are not infallible. They have made mistakes and miscalculations. The essential difference between them and us is that they recognize their mistakes rather quickly. They learn from them, draw the necessary conclusions and are quick to change their strategy or tactics when the situation requires it. They can do this because of the monolithic nature of their system, which permits a very small group of men at the top to make decisions swiftly and, where need be, radically. They do not long remain committed to a sterile, ineffective policy. If it does not produce results, they quickly switch to a different approach.

The initial miscalculation made by the Bolsheviks after their seizure of power in Russia in 1917 was their belief that revolutions would quickly follow throughout most of the rest of the world. They even considered it necessary that this should happen if the Revolution in Russia were not to be crushed by outside attack. Their expectations were soon disappointed. A Communist regime did take power briefly in Hungary but was soon overthrown. The Communist movement in Germany was smashed. The defeat of the Red Army in a war with Poland in 1920 disabused the Bolsheviks of the idea that the proletariat would automatically rise against their masters on the appearance of Soviet troops. Likewise, hopes for a rising of the backward and colonial peoples of Asia proved in vain. Throughout the 1920's, there was one failure after another of revolutionary movements outside Russia. The Soviet Union was militarily weak and was unable to give other than ideological support to the world revolution. Without power behind it, the Marxist ideology alone proved ineffective.

Stalin quickly foresaw that the Soviets must build their power base at home before they could extend the Revolution abroad. He used this thesis in his struggle for power with Trotsky after Lenin's death in 1924. The main controversy between the two was which came first—the consolidation of the Revolution at home, or the world revolution. Stalin argued the former and his policy of "Socialism in one country" was adopted by the 14th Communist Party Conference in 1926. This consolidated Stalin's victory over Trotsky and the "left deviationists." He next proceeded to crush his enemies on the right. By allowing millions of peasants to starve, Stalin eliminated the last vestiges of capitalism on the Russian steppes and made himself the absolute master of the Soviet Union.

During the 1930's, the Soviets regarded themselves as encircled by the capitalists; their diplomacy concentrated primarily on attempting to prevent any hostile coalition from forming against them while they strove mightily to build up their industrial and military power. Instead of the Soviet Union aiding the Communist parties abroad to foment revolution, it was the other way around. The mission of World Communism was to defend the Soviet Union as the revolutionary base by agitating against any hostile policy towards the U. S. S. R. The Communist parties in Europe sought to form united fronts with non-Communist parties against the menace of Fascism. Russia sought respectability within the family of nations. She generally cooperated in efforts toward disarmament and collective security as represented by the League of Nations.

During this time, the Soviets always regarded war with capitalism as inevitable. But they intended that it should come at a time of their own choosing, if possible. In 1931, Dmitri Z. Manuilsky, who later became the Ukranian delegate to the United Nations, is reported (in the notes of one of the participants) to have told the students of the Lenin School of Political Warfare in Moscow:

War to the hilt between capitalism and Communism is inevitable. Today, of course, we are not strong enough to attack. Our time will come in twenty or thirty years. In order to win, we shall need the element of surprise. The Bourgeoisie will have to be put to sleep, so we shall begin by launching the most spectacular peace movement on record. There will be electrifying overtures and unheard of concessions. The capitalist countries, stupid and decadent, will rejoice to cooperate in their own de-

48

struction. They will leap at another chance to be friends. As soon as their guard is down, we shall smash them with our clenched fist.

That war might come before the Soviets were ready for it was recognized by Stalin who gave this prescription for dealing with such a situation:

If war begins, we shall not be able to remain sitting on our hands. We shall be forced to enter it. But we must enter it last. We shall enter the war in order to throw a decisive weight on the scales and thus change the balance of power. Hence the conclusion: we must be ready for anything.[1]

In the late 1930's, the rapidly growing military power of Nazi Germany induced Stalin to try out this stratagem. If Germany could become engaged with Britain and France in a war to the death while Russia remained on the sidelines, the prospects for extending Communism over a prostrate Europe by means of Soviet military power, which was growing considerably as a result of the forced industrialization of the Five-Year Plans, were very inviting.

Viewing it in this light, we may strongly suspect that the Soviet pledge to join Britain and France in defense of Czechoslovakia at the time of the Sudetenland Crisis in 1938 was a calculated deception. It was intended as an inducement to the Western Powers to check Hitler in a war from which the Soviets would profit. Once the battle was joined, the Soviets would have found a convenient pretext for remaining inactive. The lack of a common frontier with Czechoslovakia would in any case have

49

rendered effective Soviet aid to the Czechs almost impossible.

Instead, Hitler was appeased at Munich, and a much stronger Germany trained her sights on Poland in 1939. Stalin then elected to make his notorious Non-aggression Pact with Hitler. Britain and France had given iron-clad guarantees to Poland. There was no doubt that if Hitler moved against Poland there would be war. A pact with Hitler had two advantages in Stalin's mind. It would guarantee that Hitler *would* move and thus precipitate the war which Stalin hoped would weaken capitalism. Secondly, it would assure Soviet neutrality and the opportunity to emerge in the aftermath unscathed or to join the winning side at the last moment.

It was an excellent scheme, but it was based on a serious miscalculation of German strength and intentions which nearly proved fatal to Soviet power. The conquest of France dealt a severe blow to Soviet hopes that Germany would exhaust herself on the Western front. Even so, German failure to conquer Britain immediately afterward evidently restored some degree of Soviet confidence. At a meeting with Hitler in Berlin in November, 1940, Soviet Foreign Minister Molotov engaged in some very tough bargaining with the Germans over the future division of the world. Notable was his refusal to give way to Germany in the areas which the Soviet Union considered to be within her own sphere of influence—Romania, Bulgaria, the Dardanelles, and Finland. Molotov obviously did not reckon with the effect of this stubbornness on Hitler.

What followed should be an object lesson for those

who believe that Russia can be provoked into going to war when she is not ready. After deciding on "Operation Barbarosa," Hitler made his preparations for the attack on Russia during the spring of 1941. These involved the movement of German troops into Finland and Bulgaria (areas Russia claimed to be in her sphere of influence), the German attack on Yugoslavia, with which Russia had just signed a treaty of friendship, and, of course, the concentration of huge numbers of German troops along the Soviet borders. The Soviet reaction to all of this was extremely mild. Nothing more than polite protests came from Moscow. So desperately did Stalin seek to avert the German blow that he refused to make any defensive preparations, let alone try to forestall the German attack by striking first. On the very eve of the German invasion of Russia, when the mounting intelligence indications could not be ignored, Molotov was adopting a pleading tone with the German ambassador:

There were a number of indications (Molotov told him) that the German Government was dissatisfied with the Soviet Government. Rumors were even current that a war was impending between Germany and the Soviet Union. . . . The Soviet Government was unable to understand the reasons for Germany's dissatisfaction. . . .[2]

Even Khrushchev, when attacking Stalin's ostrich-like policy of those days at the 20th Communist Party Congress in 1956, did not suggest that the Soviet Union should have forestalled the German blow by attacking first. He merely berated Stalin for his failure to take adequate defensive measures.

I have briefly recounted these main trends of Soviet thought and policy leading up to World War II in order to provide the setting for the much more important development of Soviet policy which has followed since the war. It is still the fashion of many writers on Communism to write long and ponderous studies dealing with the minutiae of Communist doctrine dating back to the original Communist Manifesto in 1848. Such studies are of interest to scholars and can be useful for gaining a historical perspective on the present period. The Manuilsky quote and Soviet policy towards Nazi Germany are mentioned because of their particular relevance to the situation today. The world is changing, however, and the present Soviet leaders have shown that they are quite capable of changing with it. They are not irrevocably wedded to slogans and doctrine which have lost their applicability to today's conditions. In the present situation the often quoted statements of Marx, Lenin, Stalin and others in the pre-Khrushchev era have lost much of their significance as a guide to current Soviet strategy. The Soviet state is no longer weak and backward, but a superpower which makes the world tremble and whose actions dominate the world stage. The Soviet people now generally support their government to a much greater degree than under Stalin. Russia is not now alone but at the head of a bloc of Communist states which includes the awakened dragon, China. The early conspiratorial techniques of the World Revolution are still used, but they have largely been supplemented by a center of raw power which is quite capable of employing material as well as ideological means for conquest.

Like their predecessors, the present Soviet leaders still

make mistakes; but the incredible success of the Communist movement since World War II suggests that their mistakes have been more in the realm of tactics than of strategy. Soviet strategy is related to their over-all analysis of the strengths and weaknesses of their enemies. In the past sixteen years, this analysis has proven to be remarkably accurate. Tactics are more often than not conditioned by opportunities of the moment, not necessarily of Soviet making. Here the Communists are more subject to error, but such errors can always be remedied with a minimum of loss.

It is Nikita Khrushchev who now stands at the pinnacle of Soviet power and thus at the head of World Communism. There are important differences between Russia and China both in the realm of ideology and strategy. These differences will be discussed in a separate chapter. In the Sino-Soviet alliance, however, power is very much respected. So long as Soviet power overshadows Chinese, as will continue to be the case for a considerable period at least, Khrushchev and not Mao Tse-tung will call the shots. It is, therefore, Khrushchev's strategy and that of his associates with which we must chiefly reckon and which we must understand with complete thoroughness if we expect to counter it successfully.

The greatest misconception still prevalent in the United States, both among the people and in the Government, is the belief that the Soviets will risk, or even initiate, war in pursuit of their objective of world domination. We have consistently credited the Soviets with a willingness to run a very high degree of risk, when nothing could be farther from the truth. In fact, the principal difference between the strategy of Khrushchev and that of Stalin is that Khrushchev has specifically ruled out *international* war as a method of conquest. Let us examine this point in detail.

A fundamental principle of Soviet policy under Stalin and under Khrushchev as well is that the security of the Soviet state comes above all else. It shall not be risked unnecessarily. To Stalin, this meant simply that war must be avoided, if at all possible, until such time as the Soviet Union and the countries within her orbit were so strong that the final battle of annihilation with capitalism could be undertaken with the prospect of complete success. After World War II, Stalin appreciated the importance of the atomic bomb, but he seems to have regarded it essentially as just another *means* of warfare, which, like poison gas, might not even be used. So long as the United States possessed a significant strategic advantage in nuclear weapons, war with the United States was unthinkable. The Soviet retreat in Iran in 1946, the backdown on the Berlin Blockade in 1949, and the request for peace talks in Korea in 1951 were evidences of Stalin's unwillingness to become involved in war directly with the United States. But he still regarded it as ultimately inevitable, and the Soviet armed forces were expanding both in quality and quantity at the time of his death. Until he was strong enough successfully to challenge the United States, Stalin sought to grab everything he could without war.

By the time Stalin's successor, Khrushchev, was firmly entrenched in 1955, it had become necessary for the Soviets to reappraise the doctrine of the inevitability of war. The enormously destructive hydrogen bomb had now been developed by both sides. United States military strategy was committed to the use of nuclear weapons in general war. There was no way in which the Soviet Union could reasonably hope to avoid extremely heavy damage at the very least if she became involved in an all-out war with the United States. Regardless of the effects on the capitalist world, such a war would inevitably threaten the existence of the Soviet Union itself—a fact which Malenkov was indiscreet enough to acknowledge in 1954.[3] Furthermore, the United States doctrine of "massive retaliation" created the strong possibility that any future Korea-type limited war which involved the United States could get out of hand and lead to general war.

The Soviets were therefore forced to conclude that the ultimate war to the death with capitalism foreseen by Lenin and Stalin was no longer valid doctrine. Accordingly, at the 20th Congress of the Communist Party of the Soviet Union, held in January–February, 1956, the Soviets renounced the fatal inevitability of war. This was a major doctrinal pronouncement which they have repeatedly defended against Chinese Communist ideological attack. In this instance, there is every reason to take the Soviets at their word. It is not in their national interest to run such a risk in the nuclear age. The renunciation of the fatal inevitability of war means not only that the Soviets do not intend to conquer us by surprise nuclear assault, but that they do not intend to launch limited wars either *so long as there is any chance that such a war could expand to general war.* This is an extremely important point which is very poorly understood by Americans: there is a widespread belief that the apparent nuclear stalemate now prevailing has increased the chances that the Soviets will initiate limited wars. In the sense that we think of limited wars as patterned after the Korean-type action this belief is very much mistaken. The Soviets take a very different view.

In discussing limited wars, which the Soviets refer to as "local" wars, their propaganda, and even their serious military authors, take the position that warfare cannot remain limited in the nuclear age. Writing in *Military Thought* in March, 1958, Major General N. Talenskiy declared:

Now, when there are ICBM's, should war be unleashed by the imperialists, it will inevitably engulf the whole world. . . . Contemporary strategy stresses with all clarity that the all-embracing nature of war is an inevitable and logical development. At present a local war can be nothing but the initial stage of a world war.

Earlier Khrushchev, in November, 1957, speaking of potential "incendiary" areas in the Middle East, Europe, Korea, Taiwan, and Vietnam, added:

The theory of so-called local or minor wars with the use of mass destruction weapons has now sprung up in the West. With such wars the imperialists want to suppress the national liberation movement and do away with governments which do not suit them; yet we must not think that under present conditions minor wars would be localized. Should such wars break out, they could soon grow into a world war.[4]

Soviet Defense Minister Malinovskiy in a speech to the Supreme Soviet in January, 1960, on the subject of the reduction of the armed forces, made this reference to limited war:

In mapping the line for the further development of our Armed Forces in connection with the reduction of their numbers, we proceed on the fact that the future war, if it is unleashed by aggressors, will be conducted with the mass use of nuclear weapons. We emphasize this because in the West now they speak and write a great deal about 'limited nuclear war', about 'tactical use of nuclear weapons', about 'measured strategy', about 'the strategy of intimidation', etc. etc. All these theories and, may I be permitted to say, 'strategies' testify that imperialists fear the inevitable retribution which they can suffer in case of attack upon the countries of the socialist camp.[5]

This Soviet line is undoubtedly aimed primarily at inhibiting Western military counteraction to Communist moves. It is, in fact, a Soviet attempt to employ "massive retaliation" in reverse—now that they, too, have a strategic strike capability. By portraying a local crisis as fraught with the danger of a major nuclear war, the Soviets hope so to arouse Western public opinion that the clamor for a peaceful solution will be irresistible. The Soviets threw the full support of their propaganda machine behind the Chinese Communist probing action at Quemoy in September, 1958. Khrushchev's letters to President Eisenhower reached a new height in truculence. In stating that an attack on Communist China would be an attack on the Soviet Union, Khrushchev warned that "mankind is again confronted with a direct threat of war" and stated that a situation existed which "no one would be able to get out of, neither you nor we, should a war break out in the Far East."[6]

All of this was intended to create the specter of general war erupting over the Quemoy issue, and the Soviets and Chinese Communists undoubtedly hoped that American determination to support the Nationalists on Quemoy would be shaken. When it became clear that the United States could not be swerved from its course, the crisis quickly subsided.

Apart from the propaganda, however, the Soviets undoubtedly appreciate the chance that any limited war could get out of control. The actual reason for the failure of the Soviets to permit or engage in limited war with the United States over Quemoy in 1958, and since that time, lies in a complex of Soviet assessments of the risks involved in the overt use of armed force versus the possibilities inherent in other forms of warfare. Involved are their assumptions regarding American policy, the chances of altering that policy through pressure from allies and neutrals, and their analysis of the actual military power position of the two blocs.

As the nuclear capabilities of the Soviet Union have grown in the past few years, the fear of war, and of running the risk of war, has steadily increased in the West. This fear has been skillfully magnified by Soviet propagandists, who insist that the Soviet Union is militarily equal or superior to, the United States. By emphasizing its military might, the Soviet Union hopes to obtain its objectives without risk of war. If this cannot be achieved, Soviet planners must be very realistic. As the United States has taken on more and more commitments, either legal or moral, American prestige has become deeply committed to making good on these commitments. Places like Quemoy or Berlin have little strategic importance but tremendous psychological significance, and they cannot be surrendered without the gravest psychological consequences. Once the decision is made to defend these areas, it becomes extremely difficult to accept a defeat, especially a military defeat.

Assuming that the Soviets analyze the American position in the same light, they must calculate that if the military forces of the United States become involved in any action, an extremely dangerous chain of events could be set in motion. If superior Communist conventional forces are brought to bear so that the United States is in danger of losing the limited war, we would be under the greatest pressure to retrieve the situation by employing tactical nuclear weapons. There would, of course, also be great pressure against such a step. The Soviets have attempted to promote such objections by claiming that there is no difference between tactical and strategic nuclear weapons. Nevertheless, despite a certain amount of success with this line of propaganda, Soviet planners cannot realistically assume that the United States is effectively deterred from the tactical use of nuclear weapons if the situation requires it.

Such reasoning must have been a primary factor in the failure of the Communists to accept limited war over Quemoy in 1958. They realized that if the United States committed itself to an all-out defense of Quemoy up to and including the use of tactical nuclear weapons, then the Chinese Communists would be fighting under relatively unfavorable conditions. They would be in no position to inflict equivalent damage on American forces. Communist China's great advantage—manpower— would have been almost useless against the United States

Navy; and her air force, as proved by the encounters with the Chinese Nationalists, had no guarantee of getting necessary air control of the Taiwan Straits. Even if Communist China had been willing to accept battle on these terms, the Soviet Union patently was not. In order to provide a reasonable prospect of victory, Russia would either have had to send in her own forces or to have turned over nuclear weapons to the Chinese Communists with the attendant risk of loss of control over the situation. A military showdown over Quemoy would, therefore, have opened up a whole series of unpleasant possibilities for the Soviets. It remains true today that the Soviets will avoid any direct military confrontation with the United States, regardless of the magnitude.

The greatest lesson to come out of all of our dealings with the Communists but which we somehow still seem not to have learned is simply this: Whenever we are both prepared to fight and willing to fight we will not have to do so.

In order to avoid the possible consequences of war, the Soviets have replaced the doctrine of the fatal inevitability of war with the strategy of "peaceful co-existence"—the most deadly and deceptive slogan ever developed by World Communism. It is of the utmost importance that we understand exactly what the Communists mean by this term.

"Peaceful co-existence" is in no sense permanent co-existence. It is simply a more subtle, indirect approach to conquest necessitated by the fact that the opponents of Communism are militarily stronger. The Communists are never bashful in stating their ultimate objective— consider, for example, Khrushchev's declaration in Alma

Ata on March 21, 1961, that "We shall be happy when the people of all countries stand under the banner of Marxism-Leninism and the Communist banner will fly over the whole planet." And his statement, "We will bury you," is known to every American.

What exactly then is "peaceful co-existence"? What do the Communists mean by the term? One of the best definitions appeared in the newspaper, *Soviet Russia:*

Peaceful co-existence is the general line of the foreign policy of both the U. S. S. R. and the other socialist countries. This does not mean, of course, peace in the class struggle between socialism and capitalism or reconciliation of the Communist with the bourgeois ideology. Peaceful co-existence means not only the existence of states with different social systems, but also a definite form of class struggle between socialism and capitalism on a world-wide scale. This form includes giving up military means for solution of controversial international questions and, at the same time, presupposes an ideological and political struggle and economic competition. Socialism need not resort to war for victory on a world-wide scale. Its ideas will inevitably win through peaceful competition.[7]

Translated, this means that the struggle shall go on as before, but that it shall be conducted exclusively on Soviet terms, that is to say, that the greatest strength of the West—the superior military power of the United States—shall be neutralized and shall not be employed as a counterweight to the spread of Communism. If we attempt any forcible opposition to Communism anywhere, we are not peaceably co-existing.

It has been said that ideas cannot be stopped by bullets and this is supposed to apply to Communism. This belief that Communism cannot be halted by force is one of the greatest myths of our time. In fact, unless there is a willingness to use force *Communism cannot be defeated anywhere,* as we are gradually learning. Communist ideology has never triumphed anywhere in the world by free choice of the people involved. Force of some type is always employed. This has been true, from the Revolution of 1917—when the Bolsheviks seized power by force and then closed down the legally elected Constituent Assembly—until the present time. The means of force vary. In the Baltic States, it was done by direct Soviet pressure and invasion. In Eastern Europe, power was seized with the aid—actual or threatened—of the Red Army. In China and Laos it was done by civil war. In North Vietnam it was done under the banner of anti-colonialism. In Cuba it was done by deception; Fidel Castro's Communist sympathies did not become obvious until after he had made Cuba into a police state and it was too late. The entire history of the Communist rise to power can be summarized thus: *a relatively small number of clever, dedicated, power-hungry men are won over to the Communist ideology and then employ some means of force to install themselves in power and rule over the majority.* Because Communism employs ideological as well as forceful means of conquest, it is unique in the history of conquest and doubly dangerous. Nevertheless, force remains the indispensible requirement for final success.

"Peaceful co-existence" does not, therefore, renounce force per se as a method of conflict. On the contrary, there is a distinction in the Communist mind between force and war. It is *international war* that they have renounced and not force. They will avoid the use of force only where it is likely to involve them in *international war*, specifically in a war with the United States.

Only such international wars are ruled out. General war and "local" (limited) wars are condemned, but civil or anti-colonial wars are not. In his speech in January, 1961, reporting on the World Communist Party meeting in Moscow, Khrushchev stated:

A word about local wars. A lot is being said nowadays in the imperialist camp about local wars, and they are even making small caliber atomic weapons for use in such wars; a special theory of local wars has been concocted. . . . A small imperialist war . . . may grow into a world thermo-nuclear rocket war. *We must therefore combat both world wars and local wars. . . .*[*]

Now a word about national liberation wars. The armed struggle by the Vietnamese people or the war of the Algerian people . . . serve as the latest examples of such wars. These wars began as an uprising by the colonial peoples against their oppressors and changed into guerilla warfare. Liberation wars will continue to exist as long as imperialism exists. These are revolutionary wars. Such wars are not only admissable but inevitable. . . .[8]

The type of force employed in Laos and South Vietnam is specifically sanctioned by the Communists because it runs virtually no risk of international war. This type of forceful expansion of Communism can in the last analysis only be halted by the use of counterforce, which the United States alone possesses. This is what "peaceful

[*] Italics added.

co-existence" is intended to prevent. Civil wars, in which the Communist side is aided from outside is in accordance with the rules of the game. American intervention in such wars is not.

The Soviet desire to avoid war does not mean that they do not intend to employ war as a weapon. On the contrary, while the nature of war in the nuclear age renders war itself no longer feasible as a means of conquest, it also renders it unnecessary in the Soviet view, since the mere threat of war can be used to achieve the same objective, provided the opponent can be convinced of the seriousness of the threat and the hopelessness of his situation. The "surrender or die" ultimatum may feature in the final act of the drama—namely, the subjugation of the United States; but this will only come after we have been thoroughly defeated and isolated in the Cold War and corrupted from within by the argument that Communism is not so bad after all, and anyway it is certainly better than death. The groundwork for this attitude is being laid today by some of our most influential and respected people. It is but a short step philosophically from saying that victory is not worth the *possibility* of war to saying that defeat, perhaps sugarcoated as "compromise," is preferable to the *certainty* of war. The ultimatum will only come if and when the Soviets are quite certain that we will surrender. In the meantime, we are warned that if we dare to oppose Communism by force, there will be war and we will be destroyed. Khrushchev remarked to Vice President Nixon in Moscow on July 24, 1959, "the choice for America is war or co-existence, and you must choose."

In order to make good on this threat, the Soviets must make it appear that there has been a fundamental change

64

in the world's military balance of power in favor of the camp of "peace" headed by themselves as against the camp of "war" headed by the United States. They must make it appear to us that the risks of forcible counter-action against Communism are too great. By playing the game of "power politics" to the hilt, and by displaying their scientific and economic achievements, they aim at convincing the world that lies between Russia and the United States that the triumph of Communism is inevitable and even desirable, and that the wise course is to get on the bandwagon. "Peaceful co-existence" aims to conceal the real Soviet fear of war by pretending that, as the champions of "peace," they are now so strong that the "imperialists" dare not unleash it. In the words of the 1960 Communist Manifesto:

The aggressive nature of imperialism has not changed. But real forces have appeared that are capable of foiling its plans of aggression. War is not fatally inevitable. Had the imperialists been able to do what they wanted, they would already have plunged mankind into the abyss of the calamities and horrors of a new world war.

But the time is past when the imperialists could decide at will whether there should or should not be war. More than once in the past years the imperialists have brought mankind to the brink of world catastrophe by starting local wars. The resolute stand of the Soviet Union, of the other socialist states and of all the peaceful forces put an end to the Anglo-Franco-Israeli intervention in Egypt and averted a military invasion of Syria, Iraq and some other countries by the imperialists.[9]

We will examine the actual military balance of power in the next chapter. It is sufficient here to say that the Soviets are using every opportunity to make it appear to the world that the threat of Soviet military intervention is the decisive factor in the outcome of every crisis. Each time they succeed in doing this, the image of an all-powerful Russia is sharpened.

In order that no miscalculation occur which would induce the United States to challenge World Communism by force of arms, the Soviets are very careful never to confront us with the type of direct threat to our security which would give us no honorable alternative to fighting. Instead, a frustrated United States is confronted with a great bowl of tapioca, a morass of ambiguity, which never seems to offer us a clear issue either morally or strategically on which to take a stand. The Soviet method is to serve up an ever changing mixture of threats and conciliation, alternating claps of thunder with rays of sunshine, while we dangle in futility on the yo-yo of hope and despair, uncertain how or when to come to grips with our enemy.

We are constantly probed for signs of weakness and indecision. Force or the threat of force is employed gingerly at first to test our reaction, with retreat routes left open if resistance is met. When the United States stands firm as at Quemoy in 1958, the Communists draw back. When our resolve is weak, as in Laos in 1960-61, the Communists are emboldened to advance, always carefully weighing the risks and always attempting to bluff us out of counteraction if possible.

As an alternative to fighting, we are always offered the opportunity to "negotiate." We are still relieved at such a prospect. We do not realize that the threats of war are empty. They have no other purpose than to bring about negotiations and to assure that the Communists will achieve some success in those negotiations.

Our own obsession with peace is thereby turned against us and made into an instrument for our defeat. As long as we will not accept the fact that the Communists will settle for nothing less than our complete destruction, we will always succumb to these offers to "negotiate." As long as our leaders tell us that our goal is "peace" instead of the destruction of world Communism, we will fall for the "peace offensive." This is the favorite trick of the Soviets and it has worked to their advantage time and again. They dig it out every time that the international atmosphere gets too hot for their comfort or when the United States threatens at last to take some strong stand against a Communist move. It is always accompanied by a backdrop of war-like threats intended to suggest the horrendous alternatives to a peaceful settlement of the issues.

To us, peace is an end in itself. To Khrushchev and his advisers, "peace" is a means towards an end—the conquest of the world. To us, negotiation implies a sincere effort to reach a settlement of differences. To the Communists, negotiation is simply a means of advancing the goal of World Communism. The status of the Communist World is never negotiable—only that of the Free World. The method of Communist negotiation is usually to ask for the whole loaf and then to make a great "concession" by accepting only half.

As Khrushchev declared to the Supreme Soviet on October 31, 1959, "The principle of peaceful co-existence of states with different social systems means non-interference in internal affairs, *the need for mutual concessions, compromises, adaptations, if you like—on both sides in the domain of interstate relations. . . .*"[10] [Italics added] But where are the Communist concessions and compromises? There are *never* any in fact, and sometimes not even in appearance. The Communists *never* negotiate in good faith in the sense that we understand the term. They *never* conclude an agreement unless in their judgment they are getting the better of it or unless, as in Korea, it is intended to save them from defeat on the battlefield.

The Berlin Crisis illustrates this Soviet technique over a protracted period of time. In November, 1958, Khrushchev raised the issue of the status of Berlin with what was interpreted as an ultimatum to the West to get out in six months. He was happy to let this stand until it became evident that we would not get out. Then he denied that any ultimatum was intended, and a Foreign Ministers conference was held in the spring of 1959. Khrushchev got no concessions but the heat was taken off the issue by Vice President Nixon's visit to Russia and Khrushchev's visit to the United States in September, 1959. Khrushchev left in the glow of the "Spirit of Camp David," evidently convinced that he would at least get some concessions at the Summit Conference scheduled for the spring of 1960. These calculations received a rude jolt in March when he visited French President De Gaulle and found no indication of a softening attitude, and again in April when some tough speeches, notably one by American Under Secretary of State Dillon,[11] convinced him that no concessions were likely to be forthcoming in the Paris Summit Conference set for May. This put Khrushchev in a serious dilemma. He had long been threatening to sign a separate peace treaty with East Germany if he did not get his way in Berlin. This was a bluff, but now that bluff was about to be called at the highest level and Khrushchev would have to put up or shut up—the last thing he wanted to do.

Under these circumstances, it is highly probable that Khrushchev was looking for some excuse to avoid or break up the Summit Conference and that he would have found some way to do it. The U-2 affair came at precisely the right time. It allowed him not only to escape from his dilemma by wrecking the conference, but to do so in a manner which cast the blame on the United States and achieved a great propaganda victory.

Many people believed Khrushchev's tirades in Paris were a prelude to action on Berlin. Among them were the East Germans, who are a bit slow witted at times, and who completely misjudged Khrushchev's motives. With the tension at a fever pitch, Khrushchev spoke in East Berlin five days after the Summit broke up. Now it was time to switch back to the theme of "negotiation." He was a model of conciliation and reasonableness. He would take no action on Berlin, he declared, until a new administration was in office in the United States and a new Summit Conference could be held. Khrushchev was content with his propaganda victory. He was content to bide his time until the West's resolve to defend Berlin could be softened. There were none more disappointed or surprised than the militant East German Communists. They, too, were not good students of Soviet strategy.

A new phase in the Berlin crisis began with Khrushchev's aide-memoire, presented to President Kennedy in Vienna, June 4, 1961. Flushed with his success in Laos, Khrushchev decided to test once more the Western resolve to fight for Berlin. Again the carrot and stick approach, now employed in classic dimensions. Khrushchev warned that hundreds of millions would die if war came. He spoke of developing a hundred megaton nuclear warhead as he resumed nuclear testing. He informed each European country in turn of the number of bombs required to destroy it. But he also called for "common sense" and "negotiations"—and in the West this was seized upon as evidence of reasonablesness! This time Khrushchev sensed that he could, at the least, sign his East German Peace Treaty without undue risk. "It is a fairy tale," he said, "that they will fight for the freedom of the Germans in West Germany if we sign a peace treaty."[12]

Khrushchev got no contradiction to this statement, so he apparently felt fairly safe in committing himself to signing the treaty. As this book goes to press, he has not yet specifically threatened to do anything else. Whether he steps up his threats will depend upon his evaluation of the Western willingness to fight in response to any harrassing moves which the East Germans may undertake after the signing of a peace treaty. Of course, a peace treaty can be only a fiction and the East Germans must be just as much Soviet puppets as they are now. They will do nothing about Berlin without specific Soviet permission. The Soviets will test the ground with threats and bluster, but they will permit the Germans to act only when they are convinced that there will be no Western military counteraction. Always, there will be the offer to negotiate. The Communist terms for a negotiated settlement will always appear reasonable. They will never be presented to us in the form of a black and white "get out or else. . . ." Rather the Communists seek some "solution" which will weaken the Western position, legally and physically. This applies particularly to the continued presence of Western troops in West Berlin. So long as they are there in substantial numbers, the East Germans cannot seize West Berlin without initiating hostilities. This they dare not do. If the troops can somehow be eliminated or greatly reduced, West Berlin could some day be seized swiftly and the West faced by a "fait accompli"; and the choice of acquiescence or initiation of hostilities would then be forced upon us. We might even be confronted with the spectacle of the East Germans seizing the city and the Soviets immediately calling upon the United Nations to prevent Western counteraction. The United Nations would probably comply. The problem continually confronting us is whether the maintenance of the "status quo" in Berlin is worth a war? Khrushchev hopes that eventually we will decide that it is not.

The Soviet strategy of "peaceful co-existence" is well adapted to the transformation of the world which has been going on at such an accelerated pace since Stalin's death. The break-up of the old colonial empires and the emergence of intensely nationalistic new states have been of great benefit to the Soviet Union. These new states have natural resentments against their former colonial masters. They have ambitious, usually dictatorial rulers, many of whom are scheming to extend their own power and influence. Soviet policy toward these countries is to do everything possible toward improving state relations, which may even include, on occasion, a disavowal of the actions of the local Communist Party. It means playing up to the ambitions and the vanity of the leaders. It means economic assistance, but of a type which will best promote Soviet political objectives, such as the selling of arms to Egypt, Indonesia, Guinea, Cuba, Afghanistan, and virtually any state which will accept them.

The concept of neutralism is, within the framework of "peaceful co-existence," a very valuable asset to the Communists. Within the "Socialist Camp" there can, of course, be no neutrals. A "neutral," then, means a net subtraction from the moral and physical strength of the "Imperialist Camp." Worse yet for the United States—given our present obsession with catering to the opinions of the neutrals—each neutral represents still one more chain fettering strong American counteraction to any Soviet move. Even the more pro-American neutrals, whose number steadily diminishes, cannot see Communism in the same terms as we do. In every international dispute they are bound to favor the Communist method for settlement, which is to negotiate us out of our position. The pro-Soviet neutrals, who are becoming steadily more numerous, can generally be counted on actively to back the Soviet position on most issues.

It is not usually necessary in the present context of Communist strategy to take physical possession of an area. The first task is to *deny* it to the United States—to make neutrals of our friends and thus eliminate our overseas complex of bases which encircle the Soviet Union and help to give us both a psychological and military advantage. The Soviet strategy for accomplishing this is to frighten our more squeamish allies, such as some of the NATO nations, with the threat of nuclear destruction if American bases are permitted on their territories, and to try to convince those who cannot be frightened (such as Turkey and some of our Asian allies) that we are unwilling or unable to defend them. They have had varying success so far with this policy, but obviously every evidence of American weakness contributes to its eventual success. Where feasible, the Communists are likely to direct their more overt efforts, such as guerilla warfare or even a coup d'état, against the friends or allies of the United States. The Soviet approach toward those countries which are already neutral is much softer. Here their policy is simply to nudge them gradually into a more and more pro-Soviet attitude by supporting the political or territorial ambitions and pet economic schemes of their leaders. Meanwhile, the body politic of the country is slowly softened up for an outright Communist takeover when it suits the over-all Soviet purpose.

This time will come. There are active Communist parties in eighty-seven countries in the world including nearly all the neutrals. In such neutrals, the Communist Party generally supports the government. Meanwhile, it busily prepares for the day when the nationalist regime will be shoved aside by the Communist revolution. The befuddled or scheming neutralist leaders who have so smugly tried to pursue their own interests by riding the back of the tiger will find that they have lost the game. They will be ousted by sudden, well-prepared coups made possible by their own myopic vision of the Communist danger and an apathetic ill-informed population convinced of Communism's inevitable triumph. Others, more nimble, will try to keep their positions by entering completely within the Communist orbit. It will be too late for them. Still others, who manage to survive the first stroke, may call on the United States for assistance. That, too, is likely to be vain, for the Communists will not come out openly until they are reasonably certain there will be no intervention.

For the time being the pro-Soviet neutral constitutes a "front" in the international sense and offers no justification for United States intervention. Throughout the entire Laotian crisis, the Soviets proclaimed that their maximum objective was merely the "neutralization" of Laos; and indeed this is all they really need so long as it is sufficiently oriented toward Communism so as to support the Communists internationally and offer no objection to the movement of guerillas and material into South Vietnam and Thailand.

The important thing for us to remember is that the Soviet target is the United States above all else, and that Soviet policy is conducted primarily with the objective of steadily weakening American power, prestige, and influence. They will not attempt the absolute Communization of any country unless they are convinced that (1) it is necessary, (2) it can be accomplished without undue risk, and (3) it will not, if successful, jeopardize more important objectives.

The Soviets are patient and calculating. It is the heart of their differences with the Chinese. They are perfectly aware of the enormous military strength of the United States, and they know that they must therefore move cautiously. Where they lack the capability to give military aid directly and easily through a common frontier, they must be especially cautious. This is one of the reasons they did not encourage the Communist Party in Iraq to try to seize power following the Nationalist coup d'état in 1958 and why they have not encouraged Castro to be too openly Communist. In both cases, they are afraid of American intervention. (The fearless Turks might still intervene in Iraq if the country went openly Communist.) The Soviets cannot be sure that attempts to bluff us out of such intervention, such as vaguely worded threats to take action if we attack Cuba, would be effective. Cuba, in particular, is a very important foothold in the Western Hemisphere. The Soviets are not anxious to see it go the way of Guatemala. The other reason is that an overtly Communist government in either Iraq or Cuba might prematurely jeopardize the larger Soviet designs in the Middle East and in Latin America. Castro has probably gone much further on the road to making Cuba an open Communist state than Khrushchev likes at this time. Khrushchev declined Castro's invitation to him to visit Cuba in 1960, which indicates that he did not want Castro's Communism to be too obvious. Soviet advice was probably instrumental in getting Castro to proclaim Cuba a Socialist rather than a Communist state after the abortive Cuban revolutionary invasion attempt in April, 1961. Socialism has a much better ring in the ears of most of the world than Communism.

Soviet policy in the Congo illustrates the expediency which dictates Khrushchev's attempts to capitalize on nationalism and anti-colonialism in promoting pro-Soviet neutralism.

The Congo crisis was not of Soviet making. The Premier of the newly independent Congo, Patrice Lumumba, was a violent African Nationalist who was already pro-Soviet in his outlook. Moscow had every reason to hope that he would serve the Soviet anti-Western cause in Africa. When Lumumba's army revolted against him in July, 1960, and Lumumba called for help from the United Nations to maintain order, the Soviets naturally backed his request. As the chaos spread, however, Lumumba became disenchanted with the United Nations, which would not help him subdue his political enemies, and turned to Russia for aid. The Soviets gladly complied, seeing an opportunity to establish a strongly pro-Soviet Congo if Lumumba won. Soviet and Czech technicians, agents, and aircraft poured into the country to aid Lumumba in his war against his enemies. As the Belgians returned to protect their nationals and their interests, Soviet propaganda seized on the opportunity to whip up anti-colonial sentiment among all Africans.

The Soviet gamble on Lumumba received a sharp setback as Khrushchev was on his way to the United States in September, 1960, to attend the meeting of the General Assembly of the United Nations. Colonel (later Major General) Mobutu deposed Lumumba in a coup and threw out the Soviet and Czech ambassadors and all Communist agents. Khrushchev, of course, was very unhappy at this turn of events, particularly because it was interpreted, correctly, as a Soviet defeat. His speech to the United Nations on September 23, 1960, reflected his sensitivity on this point. After first carefully declaring that Lumumba was a patriot and not a Communist, Khrushchev continued:

Some American and British newspapers . . . raise a hue and cry to the effect that the Soviet Union has suffered a defeat in the Congo. What can one say concerning such none-too-clever contentions? First we did not and could not suffer any defeat in the Congo *because we had no*

*troops there;** there was not and could not be any interference on our part in the internal affairs of the Congo.

Khrushchev was right about the troops. There were no
Soviet troops in the Congo because the United States
had specifically warned against such a move. To have
sent troops would have pushed matters over the thresh-
old of acceptable risk. Lumumba was cautioned by the
Soviet ambassador not to ask for Soviet troops. There is
no better testimony to the common misconceptions regarding the willingness of the Soviets to assume risks
than the belief prevalent in the summer and fall of 1960
that the Congo crisis contained a threat of World War
III. Even the imperturbable Dag Hammarskjold was
constrained to warn of such a possibility. On the contrary Soviets wanted no armed confrontation with the
United States in the Congo.

Of Soviet interference in Congolese internal affairs,
however, there has been plenty both before and after
Lumumba's overthrow. Here is where the left-leaning
neutral becomes such a valuable asset to the Soviets.
During the time Lumumba was imprisoned in his resi-
dence in Leopoldville, it was primarily Ghana, Guinea,
and the United Arab Republic which played the Soviet
game in the Congo. Both Ghana's Kwame Nkrumah and
the United Arab Republic's President Nasser sought to
bring the Congo under their own influence. Working in
general concert with the Soviet Union, they engaged in
ceaseless plots, intrigues, briberies, and other devious
means for restoring Lumumba to power. These intrigues

* Italics added.

failed—not, certainly, because of anything the United Nations did, but because of the tenacity of Mobutu in holding onto his power and eventually expelling both the Ghanaian and United Arab Republic ambassadors.

When Lumumba's Lieutenant, Antoine Gizenga, set up his own regime at Stanleyville in Oriental Province on December 13, 1960, and proclaimed that his was the lawful Congo regime, he was supported by the Soviet Union and the so-called "Casablanca" powers—Guinea, Ghana, Mali, Morocco, and the United Arab Republic, all of which lean in varying degrees towards the Soviet Union. Russia and the United Arab Republic supplied as much aid to Gizenga, via the Sudan, as they dared—or were able, since the Sudan opposed transit of her territory. After Lumumba's assassination in February, 1961, Russia and many other neutrals formally recognized the Gizenga regime. At the moment of writing, Gizenga has been appointed Vice Premier under the Central Congolese Government of Cyrille Adoula, which was formed in July, 1961. Gizenga retains his strength in Stanleyville and maintains his capacity to cause trouble. He still appears to represent the best Soviet hope for a pro-Soviet Congo. The game is by no means over.

And we are only playing the Soviet game if we accept peaceful co-existence on their terms.

IV

SOVIET MILITARY POWER:
FACT AND FICTION

A tremendous amount of effort is expended by the United States "intelligence community" in order to get as accurate a picture as possible of Soviet military strength. Conversely, a tremendous effort is made by the Russians to deny us as much information as possible. The U-2 flights over the Soviet Union were necessary because of the extraordinary Soviet security surrounding their military establishment. The Soviets have a very great advantage over us in the realm of military intelligence. They have merely to read our press and other news media in order to find out the latest American military developments and plans. Our "order of battle," that is, the numbers and types of divisions, missiles, ships and aircraft, is an open book. Our military strategy is freely analyzed and debated. The Soviets have a very complete knowledge of the military strength of the United States. The United States, on the other hand, must painstakingly dig out even the most basic items of military intelligence on the

Soviet Union. Our intelligence on Soviet military power is good, but it is far from perfect. There are important gaps.

Lack of precise intelligence on Soviet military strength and capabilities has caused both the United States Government and the American public seriously to overestimate the military power of the Soviet Union in relation to that of the United States and, consequently, the Soviet willingness to risk war. Such an overestimate on both counts at the highest level in 1951 brought about the ruinous decision by the United States not to fight the Korean War to a conclusion—on the grounds that to do so might bring Russia into the war. As we look back at that period, such an assumption appears ridiculous. Yet it did not appear so to the "experts" at the time.

When a nation does not have an exact picture of its potential enemy's strength, simple prudence demands that its leaders take into account the worst possibility in mapping their own plans. While this usually leads to the healthy result of strengthening one's own military forces to meet any possible attack, in the present circumstances it is strengthening the Soviets in their attempts to bluff the United States out of taking stronger military measures against the insidious step-by-step advance of World Communism.

As we have seen, Soviet strategy is to communize the world without war, but to employ the threat of war as the only alternative to "peaceful co-existence." Barring an accident or a last-ditch desperation attack on the Soviet Union by the United States—possibilities which they must obviously take into account—the Soviets never intend to use their armed forces in actual combat against the West. The "battles" in the type of war they are waging are to be won, wherever possible, at the conference table. In this type of "battle," one ICBM can do the work of fifty, at infinitely less expense, *providing the enemy can somehow be convinced that the fifty actually exist*. Obviously, the Soviets stand to profit if their military strength is exaggerated by their opponents.

Although establishment of a new Defense Intelligence Agency was announced in August, 1961, military intelligence on the Soviet Union is currently handled primarily by five organizations in the United States Government— the intelligence branches of the Army, Navy, and Air Force; the National Security Agency; and the Central Intelligence Agency. The latter has the responsibility for coordinating the outputs of the service agencies and synthesizing them into a finished product. The most important of these is the National Intelligence Estimate. This document is the estimate of potentially hostile forces which the President and National Security Council must take into account in making their decisions. Although efforts are made to resolve the differing service estimates of Soviet military strength, they are often unsuccessful—with the result that the final product usually contains important footnotes in which one or more agencies disagree with the opinions of the majority.

If these differences of opinion were always honest, they would at least be tolerable. Unfortunately, this is not always the case. The same raw intelligence information is available throughout the "intelligence community." The differing interpretations and analyses stem at least in part from the interest which each of the military services has in furthering its own parochial interests. When precise information on Soviet strength is lacking, each of the American military intelligence organizations has a tendency to exaggerate the strength and importance of the opposite military service in the Soviet Union in order that its parent service will not lose out in the jockeying for position which goes on ceaselessly between the United States Army, Navy, and Air Force. Intelligence analysts generally produce an honest and objective product until or unless they find themselves involved in a matter which could have political consequences for their own service. Then they must tread carefully. It is not a question of deliberate falsification of fact. Rather, the analyst finds that when confronted with an uncertain situation which is open to interpretation (particularly in the realm of estimating future developments) he must come up with an analysis which is at least not hostile to the "party line" of his own service.

As a result of this unhealthy situation, we have been aiding the Soviets in perpetuating one of history's greatest deceptions. They have largely succeeded in convincing the world in general and the United States public in particular that the balance of military power has swung from the West to the Soviet Union, or, at the very least, that we no longer possess military superiority. This has been one of the most important facets in their plan to conquer the world through "peaceful co-existence." The world and the American public are extremely gullible. They tend to accept Soviet boasts at face value. This is why Soviet propagandists, and Khrushchev personally, repeatedly hit the theme of Soviet military strength. If the American public believes we have lost our military superiority, it will not support a strong foreign policy. In order to carry off this fraud and assure that most people accept their claims, it is necessary for the Soviets to maintain such a state of uncertainty about their actual strength that their assertions cannot be officially denied. Secrecy and deception are all important.

This effort has largely succeeded. *Because of the political factors influencing the production of intelligence the United States Government has been laboring under a somewhat unrealistic picture of the true balance of military power.*

In order to understand present-day Soviet military developments, it is first necessary to go back to the end of World War II and put ourselves in the position of Stalin and his associates as they surveyed the post-war scene. Germany, the only land power capable of directly menacing the Soviet Union or of opposing an advance into Europe, was in ruins. The menace of the Japanese Manchurian Army in the Far East had been removed. The chief military obstacle to Soviet plans—after the rapid demobilization of the American Army in Europe— was the sea and air power of the United States, and to a much lesser degree, Great Britain.

Although Stalin's armies could easily have overrun Western Europe from 1946 on, he dared not press matters to an immediate military showdown because of his strategically inferior position. Even if he seized Western Europe, he had no means, naval or air, for defeating his maritime opponents. America's possession of the atomic bomb, combined with a strategic bomber force, which Stalin totally lacked, would have subjected the terribly war-weary Soviet people and the already devastated So-

83

viet economy to a strain which would have been unbearable. Stalin obviously could not risk war in the immediate post-war period.

Still, he believed firmly that capitalism could not finally be liquidated without war. He believed, furthermore, that this war would not be greatly different from World War II, despite the existence of the atomic bomb, which he spared no efforts to obtain for himself. In 1942, Stalin laid down the dictum that what he called the "permanently operating factors" would determine the outcome of war. These factors were the "stability of the rear, the morale of the army, the quantity and quality of divisions, the armament of the army, the organizational ability of the army commanders." He specifically denied that the factor of surprise could determine the outcome of the war. He used the failure of the initial German offensive against Russia to prove his point.

Stalin reaffirmed his dictum on the "permanently operating factors" in 1946, and it remained in effect as official Soviet doctrine until his death in 1953. In the meantime Stalin set out to build up the types of armed forces which he would need for an eventual showdown with his now principal enemy, the United States.

In Stalin's thinking, Western Europe with its tremendous population and industrial power was still very much the key to victory. What he needed was the ability not merely to seize Western Europe—if it could not be subverted—but also successfully to stand off the United States by neutralizing its sea and air power. If we could not contest the seizure of Western Europe by projecting our power overseas as we had done in World War II, we would presumably be forced to make peace. Russia would then consolidate and exploit her hold on Eurasia preparatory to a final assault on the last great citadel of capitalism. Perhaps the German employment of the V-2 rockets suggested to Stalin how the United States could eventually be brought to its knees. The feverish Soviet efforts to round up German rocket experts and the crash effort which went into the development of Soviet rockets immediately after the war is evidence of Stalin's early appreciation of their eventual usefulness.

The massive Soviet armies of World War II were only partially demobilized. These had to be ready to take care of any ground opposition when Stalin gave the word to attack. Meanwhile, by their very existence, they made a hostage of Western Europe and could serve as a deterrent to any American temptation to take advantage of its atomic monopoly. The formation of NATO and above all the specter of German rearmament were always potential, though as it turned out, never very real threats to an easy Soviet drive to the English Channel. A cardinal feature of Soviet diplomacy in the early 1950's was to prevent, if possible, any really strong ground force from arising to oppose her in Europe. As a counter to NATO, the Soviets formed the Warsaw Pact in May, 1955, placing the Soviet and European satellite armies under one command. This had little real significance other than to give the Soviets a bargaining lever in their efforts to neutralize NATO.

Russia made little effort to develop a strategic bombing force until the early 1950's, after she had developed the atomic and hydrogen bombs. To do so earlier would have made little sense. She did build a few hundred copies of a captured U. S. B-29 bomber (the "BULL") as an interim measure, which gave her a one-way bombing capability against the United States. These were slow, prop-driven aircraft, however, whose capabilities were largely psychological. Beginning in 1955, the Soviets began to put in service jet-propelled "BISON" and turbo-prop "BEAR" heavy bombers. Although subsonic, these aircraft gave the Soviet Union for the first time a significant bombing capability against the United States. As such, they caused a consternation greatly disproportionate to the actual threat they posed. By the time they went into production, the Soviets were deep in the process of re-evaluating their whole politico-military strategy, in which they valued the bombers chiefly for their deterrent value until they could be supplemented by ICBM's. The bombers were ostentatiously displayed to Western observers during the May Day celebrations in Moscow in 1955 and 1956. Our intelligence took the bait and estimated a much higher production rate than proved to be the case.

Perhaps the most significant clue to Stalin's concept of future war was the post-war development of the Soviet Navy. Under the leadership of Stalin's protégé, Admiral Nikolai Kuznetsov, the Soviets set about building a navy after World War II which would be capable of challenging Anglo-American naval power not only beneath the sea but on the surface as well. By the late 1940's, Soviet shipyards had been repaired and were engaged almost exclusively in naval construction. Of major importance was the submarine fleet. Although it cannot be verified, Admiral Kuznetsov was reported to have set the goal in 1948 at 1,200 submarines. The Soviets concentrated their production on long-range types capable of operating on the North Atlantic shipping lanes with a few able to operate off the coasts of the United States for nuisance value. Their major objective, obviously, was to prevent American reinforcements from reaching Europe during or after a Soviet attack. By 1956, the total number of Soviet submarines was approaching 500, over half of which were snorkel-equipped, post-World War II construction.

Besides favoring submarines, Admiral Kuznetsov was an advocate of a large surface fleet which would be able to protect Soviet shores against hostile naval forces and eventually operate on the high seas. Towards this end, large numbers of destroyers and the Sverdlov class of cruisers were built in the early 1950's. The Sverdlovs were an intelligence puzzle. Large (20,000 tons) "light" cruisers (6″ gun main battery), their extended cruising ranges made them suitable for high-seas operations and yet, unsupported by carriers, they would have little chance to survive even as commerce raiders in the era of modern air power. Carriers were expected (and officially estimated) to follow, but no Soviet aircraft carriers ever appeared. When all other navies had abandoned construction of conventional cruisers, the Soviet interest in them seemed doubly strange.

There is now evidence that the Sverdlovs were indeed intended as a first step towards the creation of a high-seas surface fleet which would have included even larger "heavy" cruisers and, as a final step, aircraft carriers. These Soviet squadrons would bear great similarity to the American carrier strike fleets of World War II. Thus, the entire Soviet naval program of the early post-war years testifies particularly to Stalin's feeling that war with the Western Powers was inevitable and to his still somewhat archaic concepts of how that war would be fought, that is, as a war of attrition with conventional military forces. The naval program was a tremendous drain on Russian resources. It seems unlikely that these huge numbers of ships would have been built if there was no intention of using them.

There are indications that Stalin was beginning to modify his thinking somewhat even before he died. The 19th Communist Party Congress held in October, 1952, made no mention of the inevitability of war and stressed peaceful competition of differing social systems. What is certain is that Stalin's successors made a thorough reappraisal of the question of war. Having once decided that war was no longer feasible or necessary to communize the world, they undertook sweeping changes in their military posture as well.

It is unlikely that the decision to renounce the fatal inevitability of war was made before 1955, when Khrushchev overthrew Malenkov as Premier and gradually entrenched himself as the dominant figure in the collective leadership. Prior to that time, in 1953-55, there was relative freedom of expression for the professional Soviet military leadership. In a series of articles in the Soviet press, a new military doctrine emerged. Stalin's dictum of the "permanently operating factors" was overthrown, and the factor of surprise in nuclear warfare was acknowledged to be of at least crucial, if not decisive, importance to the outcome of a war.

Khrushchev seems to have adhered to this professional military opinion. It fitted in nicely with his plans to reduce and streamline the Soviet military establishment to make it conform to the new Soviet strategy of "peaceful co-existence." Once the decision was taken not deliberately to initiate general war against the West, actual military superiority even if it could be achieved—and against the United States this was highly doubtful—made little sense. If the enemy struck first, the superiority might quickly be wiped out. Khrushchev's real purpose was to avoid nuclear war. Basically what he needed then was a *deterrent* force, strong enough to discourage any desperation attack on the Soviet Union and strong enough also to at least neutralize American military superiority by means of a pre-emptive surprise attack if worse came to worst and the Soviets concluded that a war not of their choosing was imminent and unavoidable.

Khrushchev's ideas have altered very slightly as of this writing, and this is chiefly in regard to "surprse attack." In a major pronouncement on Soviet military doctrine, delivered to the Supreme Soviet on January 14, 1960, he denied that "any country" would derive decisive advantage by launching a surprise attack against a large nuclear power.[1] He stressed that the Soviet Union would henceforth rely almost entirely on its missile forces as a deterrent (he even used this word) to any attack on the Soviet Union. This suggests that Khrushchev, as a realist, acknowledged that against the increasingly mobile American strategic striking forces even a pre-emptive attack would offer little hope of success. Everything depends on deterring an American attack in the first place. If he is to succeed in his grand design for World Communism, it is absolutely imperative that he avoid nuclear war.

This is the basis of actual Soviet military policy today.

Their aim is to avoid actual war. They will fight the United States *only if they themselves are attacked.* But they intend to pursue their objective of world domination by the methods outlined in the previous chapter in safety by convincing the United States and the world that they are much stronger than is in fact the case and that therefore we have no choice other than to accept their definition of "peaceful co-existence." This is where their military secrecy is so all important. They know full well that if they can keep us and the world guessing concerning certain key elements of their military strength, we will inevitably credit them with a much stronger position than would be the case if we knew all the facts. They can thereby achieve a deterrent without crippling their economy to do it.

Exactly what then is fact and what is fiction?

This much is fact: between late 1955 and at least the end of 1960 there was a gradual reduction of over two million men in the armed forces. Khrushchev declared, in his January, 1960, speech that the armed forces stood at 3,623,000 and that there would be a further reduction of 1,200,000 men in the next two years. That statement was probably accurate to the extent that it reflected Soviet personnel strength and intentions at that time. Throughout 1960 there were intelligence indications that the additional personnel cuts were taking place; however, there were also indications that professional Soviet military leaders were unhappy with the cuts. There was much dissatisfaction among officers who found themselves suddenly uprooted from comfortable positions.

The production of the BISON and BEAR heavy bombers was never great—considerably less than 200 put in service—and has largely ceased. Prototypes of other bombers were built during the late 1950's but they were not produced in quantity. The total number of Soviet aircraft actively in service was substantially reduced— particularly in 1960—from almost 20,000 to less than 15,000.

The quantitative build-up of the Soviet Navy came to a halt after the mid 1950's. Admiral Kuznetsov was replaced in 1955 by Admiral Gorshkov, and Kuznetsov's big ship program was scrapped. The plan for aircraft carriers was abandoned on the reasoning that it would take the Soviets many years to perfect such ships and that they might then be obsolete. With no carriers planned, the projected "heavy" cruisers made no sense and the Sverdlov class of "light" cruisers became militarily almost useless. Khrushchev confirmed this when, after traveling on a state visit to Britain in April, 1956, aboard the cruiser *Ordzhonikidze*, he declared: "Under modern war conditions, the best thing that cruisers can be used for is to carry guests to a friendly country and to fire salutes." The Sverdlov building program ceased in 1955, with at least four ships only partially completed. These were all scrapped in 1960. The submarine program reached its peak in 1956 when nearly 100 units were built and has fallen off sharply since that time. The construction of destroyers also underwent a marked slowdown. Many of the principal shipyards hitherto engaged in naval construction are now producing merchant ships.

The decreased emphasis on conventional military forces after 1955 was accompanied by a reorientation of the Soviet armed forces towards missile and nuclear warfare. The first surface-to-air anti-aircraft missiles were available about 1955 and were emplaced in rings around Moscow. Short range tactical surface-to-surface missiles were introduced into the Soviet Army about 1956, and the first 1,000 mile range surface-to-surface missile was possibly operational in about 1957.

New developments in the Navy were much slower in coming. This is probably because the Navy was relegated to a secondary position in the Soviet system of military priority. The first conventionally powered missile-firing submarines did not become operational until at least 1959. Unlike our POLARIS submarines, they must surface in order to fire their missiles, which are of relatively short range. The Soviets have had considerable difficulty with the power plant of their nuclear icebreaker LENIN, and this may explain why their nuclear submarine program has been delayed. It is probable that the Soviets now have some nuclear-powered submarines, as they claim, and a POLARIS type would be a logical development. However, despite their claims to the possession of nuclear-powered, missile-armed submarines none has yet been shown publicly. Certainly they are far behind the United States in their submarine program. The principal surface ship is apparently to be the guided-missile destroyer which the Soviets call a "cruiser." The first of these were put in service in the late 1950's and displayed to the world in the naval parade at Leningrad in July, 1961. Missile-armed torpedo boat types were also revealed.

The key to Soviet nuclear blackmail and the only really effective weapon capable of striking the United States is the Intercontinental Ballistic Missile—the ICBM. This has been the one category of weapons in which the Soviet

Union has plainly been ahead of the United States up to the present time. It is the most important element of Soviet military strength and the element which lends itself most easily to deception. The actual number of Soviet ICBM's is unknown, and the Soviets carefully keep it so.

What *is* known is that the first prototype ICBM was fired on a test range in August, 1957, well ahead of the United States. It is also known that ICBM's were very accurately fired, also from a testing station, to an impact area in the Central Pacific in February, 1960. The Soviets made no secret of these successes. What is not so well known (by the public) is that the Soviets have also experienced many failures in their ICBM program (as well as in their space program) and that their ICBM was probably not *operational,* that is, ready to be used in war even in very small numbers until at least 1960, if then. It is certain that Khrushchev does not have nearly as many as he would like us to believe.

The most important element of fiction in Soviet military strength concerns the way in which they have exploited their limited but very dramatic achievements in missilery and space to bluff the entire world into believing that they have become invincible. The Soviets are not eight feet tall. They only seem that way. Their scientists are brilliant, but they do not yet exist in great depth. The Soviet economy, though gaining, is still far behind the United States. "Crash" programs, such as the development of the ICBM and the man in space, cannot be achieved without a great drain on talent and resources and the sacrifice of other programs. The United States space program, for example, though behind the Soviets in booster rockets and thus in the capability to lift huge tonnages into orbit, nevertheless possesses a depth and diversity which the Russians lack. They, therefore, concentrate first on the programs which will create the maximum psychological impact and can best be exploited for political purposes.

The exploitation of the first ICBM shot in August, 1957, illustrates the Soviet "half truth" technique. The Communist Party newspaper, *Pravda*, announced the feat with much fanfare on August 27, 1957, declaring:

The results achieved indicate that it is possible to send missiles to any part of the world. The solution of the problem of the creation of intercontinental ballistic missiles permits the reaching of distant regions, without resorting to strategic aviation, which at the present time is vulnerable to the modern methods of anti-aircraft defense.

Pravda thus implied a Soviet capability to strike the United States, while questioning the American capability to hit Russia with our "vulnerable" SAC forces.

Following the launching of the first Sputnik on October 4, 1957, Khrushchev wasted no time in pushing home the advantage. In an interview with James Reston, *New York Times* correspondent, on October 7, 1957, Khrushchev cited Sputnik as proof of the Soviet ICBM capability:

I think I will not be revealing any secrets if I tell you that we now have all the missiles we need: Long-range missiles, intermediate-range missiles and short-range missiles . . . these means fully insure our defense.[2]

To William Randolph Hearst he said in an interview on November 22, 1957:

The Soviet Union possesses ICBM's. It has different missile systems for various missions; all our missiles are built so that they can be equipped with atomic and hydrogen warheads. . . .[3]

These statements suggested that the missiles were on the firing line and ready to go, but in fact they were made when the Soviets were not even close to possessing an operational ICBM! This fact is a significant indication of the extent to which Soviet propaganda regularly exceeds Soviet reality.

The possibilities inherent in the submarine as a weapon of strategic attack, and thus of deterrence and intimidation, were not overlooked either. Air Marshall Constantine Vershinin, in an interview published on September 8, 1957, declared:

The submarine fleets have now become a formidable weapon. They can bombard coastal cities—and not only coastal cities. They can bombard other objectives with rocket weapons with atomic or hydrogen warheads.[4]

And Khrushchev hit the same theme in an interview with United Press Correspondent Henry Shapiro on November 14, 1957:

It is true that we are surrounded by American bases. But we have our intercontinental ballistic missile rockets and submarines. [It is possible to keep] all of America's vital centers under fire from submarines with the help of ballistic missiles and to blockade the U. S. coasts.[5]

The prototypes of Soviet missile-firing submarines may have been under construction when these statements were made, but a significant operational capability was still years away. Yet the Soviets spoke as if such a capability existed at that moment.

I have cited these examples of Khrushchev's efforts to obtain credit for a military capability which he did not possess in order to demonstrate to the reader that the Soviet Union consistently exaggerates its military strength. Examples of such Khrushchev braggadoccio have been legion in the years since 1957. He does not usually lie in such a manner that he can be proved to be lying. In his discourses on Soviet military prowess, there is always some element of fact—but coupled with a conclusion or inference drawn from that fact which is almost totally false. Khrushchev's objective is not only to mislead world opinion, including prominent and influential people in the United States, into thinking that America has lost its military dominance; it is also to fool, where possible, the intelligence services of the West. To do this, he must combine a fact which can be verified with an assertion which cannot. One of the best examples of this technique occurred at a Kremlin reception for Soviet journalists on November 14, 1959. Khrushchev boasted at length on Soviet missile capabilities:

I think, dear comrades, members of the Presidium, that I will not reveal a secret—and at the same time I want to be understood correctly: *We do not want to frighten anyone,** but the truth we can say—that now we have accumulated such a quantity of missiles, such a quantity of atomic and hydrogen warheads that, if they attack us, we could wipe all our potential enemies off the face of the earth. . . . During a visit to one of the plants, we learned how the workers, engineers and scien-

* Italics added.

tists produce missiles. . . . In one year that plant which we visited produced on the assembly line 250 missiles with hydrogen warheads.[6]

So here is Khrushchev claiming the power to wipe all his enemies—including of course the United States—off the face of the earth, and claiming the figure of 250 missiles produced at one plant to prove his point. He must have known the bombshell this would throw into the Pentagon. He realizes that we know he "has" the ICBM and a family of smaller missiles in the sense that he has developed the weapon systems. He also knows that we do not know exactly how many missiles he has. Therefore, he is free to make extravagant claims and even mention a figure of 250—and he does not specify what type of missiles they are—since there is no way of accurately checking up on him. Although we have no confirmation of the statement, our tendency, given lack of specific knowledge, will be to give at least *some* credence to the claim. So goes Khrushchev's strategy of bluff.

This attempt at nuclear blackmail emphatically rejects for public consumption any idea that nuclear war would destroy both antagonists. As mentioned earlier, one of Malenkov's sins, during his brief reign as Premier in 1953-55, was his assertion that both sides would be destroyed by nuclear war. Such an idea has no part in Khrushchev's public doctrine. Khrushchev admits that the Soviet Union would suffer losses in a thermonuclear war, but claims that she would survive because her population and industry is less concentrated than in the West. Capitalism, he confidently claims, would be completely destroyed. The threat of war as an alternative to "peaceful co-existence" will only work if the Soviets can make the world believe they are not afraid of it. The fact is, however, that they *are* afraid of it; they do not wish it; they will not start it. Thus, their entire psychological offensive is a gigantic fraud.

Soviet military policy since 1955 has had one central objective: to support the over-all strategy of "peaceful co-existence" by neutralizing the tremendous military superiority of the United States. An attempt to do this by means of an arms race in the usual sense would be futile since they would be pitted against us in the fields of technology and economic resources—still our greatest strengths. Instead, they have taken one area in which they are ahead of us—booster rockets—and with consummate skill have largely succeeded in achieving *political* neutralization of United States military power. They have done this while possibly *reducing* their military expenditures because of the sharp cutback in their conventional military forces. These cutbacks were accompanied by a steady barrage of propaganda about the Soviet Union's "peaceful" intentions—but also by pointed warnings that the capabilities of the Soviet armed forces were actually increasing because of their conversion to missile armament.

On July 8, 1961, Khrushchev announced that the Soviet Union was increasing its military spending by 3.5 billion dollars and was halting the reductions in the Soviet armed forces which had been announced in January, 1960. Speaking in the contexts of the Berlin situation and disarmament, Khrushchev blamed the United States and NATO for failing to match unilateral Soviet disarmament and for increasing its strength. He also complained that the West was not drawing the proper conclusions from Soviet military strength:

Today it is acknowledged in the West that the forces of the Soviet Union and the other Socialist countries are not inferior to the forces of the Western powers.

*However, the proper conclusions are not drawn from this fact:** Given equal forces there must also be equal rights and equal opportunities. Yet our partners, acknowledging that the balance of power has tilted not in their favor, nevertheless want to dominate in international agencies and impose their will there.[7]

The next day, July 9, the Soviets put on a spectacular display of air power for the benefit of Western observers. Two new jet bombers were displayed, as well as new fighters and several other types of aircraft.

It is evident from the timing of Khrushchev's announcement of increased defense expenditures and the air display that they were intended to exert psychological pressure on the West in relation to the Berlin crisis. Some tangible evidence was needed to remind the world of Soviet strength. Beyond this, it is pertinent to examine the meaning of this seeming reversal of Soviet military policy.

The new aircraft were all developed long before the Berlin crisis was developed. The delta wing "BOUNDER" heavy bomber existed in prototype at least as far back as 1958 but was never shown until 1961. Some of the other aircraft were not really "new" but merely modifications of older aircraft. The bombers, in particu-

* Italics added.

lar, are now equipped with air-to-surface missiles. The essential question is whether the Soviets will now resume production of heavy bombers in significant quantities. This is not yet certain; evidence of it is still lacking. Khrushchev has frequently asserted that manned aircraft are obsolete, particularly in his January, 1960, speech. The aircraft shown at Tushino in July, 1961, had all been developed or were under development when he made these claims. While the ICBM was still being tested, the development of new bomber types was only elementary military prudence. If production of long range heavy bombers is now to be resumed, it can only mean that the Soviets have considerable doubts as to the *military* usefulness of their ICBM as a strategic weapon. Khrushchev must take the opinions of his military professionals into some account. These gentlemen, who must always reckon on the possibility of actual war, may be unwilling to rely exclusively on a weapon which can destroy cities but which has proven to lack the reliability and accuracy necessary to destroy military targets. The bomber possesses this reliability and accuracy, but its vulnerability, particularly to the Soviets who are at a geographic disadvantage, is a fact. If they now feel constrained to build up a heavy bomber force, it is a sign of weakness and not of strength.

Similarly, the cancellation of personnel reductions— if real and not just propaganda—is probably a sign that the dissatisfaction of Russian military leaders with those cuts has become acute. As prudent military men, they want more of the substance as well as the appearance of military power.

Khrushchev is, of course, mindful of the fact that the

vaunted military superiority of the Soviet Union is much more political than actual. For this reason, his call for general and complete disarmament is genuine to a degree. Since the Soviet Union is in fact the weaker party, Khrushchev logically reasons that even a substantial degree of nuclear disarmament would negate the American military advantage and give him an even freer hand to push the development of his civilian economy and various paramilitary operations abroad. It would not, for example, hinder such operations as the Communist penetration of Southeast Asia, but it might render the United States powerless to intervene to stop these operations. (It would also have a seriously dislocating effect on the American economy. Despite official disclaimers, no economist not dependent on the government for his livelihood denies the fact that a sudden major reduction in defense expenditures would have at least temporarily acute economic consequences.) Khrushchev cannot, however, agree to the West's condition for disarmament, which is to set up adequate control machinery before disarmament is actually carried out. The myth of Soviet military superiority depends entirely on secrecy. Khrushchev fears that if the true picture of Soviet military strength were known, his bluff would be exposed and the United States, realizing Russia's threats of war were empty, would cease further disarmament and change her foreign policy to a far tougher line. Khrushchev is thus on the horns of a dilemma. Despite the advantages to him of disarmament, an effective control system would more than outweigh them. To Khrushchev, our demand for control first and disarmament second is just camouflage for legalized espionage. What is important to understand, however, is that *his sensitivity on this point is explainable only on the grounds that it would expose Soviet weakness and not strength.*

The Soviet Union today possesses a very powerful military establishment. She is second only to the United States in military power, but she is definitely *second.* The United States is by no means a "second class" military power, and we are not on the road to becoming one —except in our own imaginations. The American people, and many of our leaders, have become virtually obsessed in recent years by the question of the so-called "missile gap"—the difference in the number of ICBM's possessed by the United States and Russia. Soviet superiority in the number of ICBM's is very probably not so great and most certainly not so significant as is commonly believed. In actuality, there may be no "gap" at all. Soviet heavy bombers, few in number, would have to travel thousands of miles across territory dominated by hostile military forces. Soviet conventionally powered missile-firing submarines are very vulnerable to submarine countermeasures. Russia's entire conventional submarine force of about 400 boats is being threatened with obsolescence because of the remarkable technological improvements being made in antisubmarine warfare.

The ICBM, then, still remains Russia's only effective weapon for damaging the United States. The most pessimistic estimates of Soviet ICBM strength were never supported by intelligence but were predicated on unsubstantiated and politically inspired estimates of Soviet intentions. This is the principal reason for overestimating Soviet strength: United States policy-makers tend to calculate on the basis of the most pessimistic estimate.

The strength of the United States vis-à-vis the Soviet Union rests on far more than a statistical comparison of military hardware. The ICBM is only one of a whole spectrum of weapons with which we can hit the Soviet Union. Our own manned aircraft, operating from bases or carriers close to the borders of the Soviet Union, or even from the United States, would still be able to get through to their targets in significant numbers. Former Secretary of Defense Gates pointed out on December 10, 1960, that American reconnaissance planes had "riddled" Soviet air defenses for the past four years—a reference to the U-2 and other flights.[8] The very vastness of Soviet territory and the many avenues for our attack make its air defense—even with missiles—very difficult. Interception cannot begin until the aircraft are near or over Soviet territory. Such developments as the long-range air-to-surface missile work more to the advantage of the United States than to the Soviet Union. Intermediate-range missiles, such as THOR in Britain, MACE in West Germany, and JUPITER in Turkey and Italy give the United States an advantage which Russia cannot match. Our POLARIS submarines, now a going concern, are virtually impossible for Russia to counter. They can remain submerged in waters over which the Soviet Navy has little or no control. On the other hand, even if and when the Soviet Navy develops a POLARIS-type submarine, it must still operate in waters controlled by hostile naval forces and will be vulnerable to submarine countermeasures. Here again geography and not merely numbers works for the United States.

Neither is there any intelligence evidence that the

Soviet Union is attempting, at this time, to create a really huge missile arsenal capable of devastating the United States. We have only Khrushchev's word for it. It is the same problem of capability versus intention. Russia has the capability to build a huge missile stockpile if she wished to make the effort, but there is no real evidence that she is doing so. Unless Russia planned to attack us, such a policy would make little sense. Despite Soviet secrecy, a really crash program to build up a very large ICBM capability could not be entirely concealed and would provoke a countereffort by the United States. Her absolute capacity to damage the United States would increase, of course, but her own destruction would be just as certain and war would not be any more attractive as a method of conquest. The effects of such a build-up would be largely negative, from the Soviet viewpoint. Her economic growth would be held back by such an extremely expensive program, and the chances of a desperation attack by the United States, prompted by the ominous intelligence indications, might even increase. It is scarcely surprising, then, that the Soviets have chosen the course of deterrence in their military policy. For them, such a policy can be just as effective when the forces behind it are partly fictitious as when they are actual.

We have seen this policy in action for the past six years. What the Soviets have done is to concentrate their best scientific and military brains on the development of new weapons systems, but they have not produced these weapons in quantity beyond what they consider the minimum needs of their defense. Meanwhile, they have used their space program and ICBM shoots into the Pacific as ostentatious "proof" of their invincible military capabilities. It is the greatest "con" game of modern times. They are playing largely on our fear of the unknown.

We may expect a continuation of this Soviet policy until such time as they have won the Cold War and driven us at last back to our own homeland. Then they may elect to produce the weapons systems of that day in great quantity in order to create the overwhelming military superiority necessary to back up the "surrender or die" ultimatum which will be intended to accomplish our "peaceful" subjugation. Until that time, they will continue to bluff—now and again coming up with some new scientific achievement to "prove" their invincibility. Soviet development of an anti-ICBM missile would be one development to anticipate for the future. If the Soviets should develop this sooner than we develop the NIKE ZEUS anti-ICBM missile, the propaganda value to them would be enormous. But sooner or later both sides will develop such a counterweapon and what will then happen to the Soviet ICBM threat? This is another reason why they do not want to be caught with too large a stockpile of obsolete ICBM's.

Finally, there are intangible factors in the military equation which transcend, perhaps, both statistics and geography. The European satellite armies are not only uncertain assets for the Soviets—they are potential liabilities. Given the proper psychological stimulus, these armies could revolt against their Russian masters if war came. The morale of Soviet servicemen is none too certain. In World War II, more than 300,000 Red Army men, headed by General Vlassov, defected to the Germans. The military effectiveness of the Soviet armed forces is almost certainly adversely affected by the constant tug of war between the "political officer" and the professional. Marshall Zhukov's dismissal as Defense Minister in 1957 was motivated at least in part by his efforts to reduce the activities of political officers in the armed forces. And there are the Soviet people themselves, increasingly proud of their country's achievements but more and more fearful that another war would jeopardize what they have won. They would have little enthusiasm for a war waged for the purpose of imposing Communism outside the Soviet Union.

The facts versus the fiction of Soviet military power lead to these conclusions: First, the military "stalemate" is a fraud. The military facts of life add up to a mockery of Khrushchev's boasts of superiority or even equality. Overwhelming military power continues to lie with the United States. If war came, we would win. Second, in any direct confrontation between the Soviet Union and the United States, in which the possibility of international war exists, *the Soviet Union will back down,* unless the United States foolishly lets itself be bluffed into doing so first. We have allowed ourselves to fall into the trap of believing that United States military opposition to Communist moves would involve the risk of all-out war. In fact, such risk is virtually zero. It is the risk of *inaction* which is a hundred times more real and a hundred times more deadly. All too often we have accepted this risk and we are paying the penalty for it.

V

RUSSIA AND CHINA

In the discussion in Chapter III of Khrushchev's methods for bringing about the world victory of Communism, only brief mention was made of the differences which he has encountered with his Chinese allies over this question. The reader was promised a separate discussion of this matter in support of the thesis that Communist global strategy is, in the last analysis, determined in Moscow and not in Peiping, regardless of the extent of Chinese disagreement. Such a discussion is now in order.

The relationship between the Soviet Union and Communist China is a complex one, and much more is involved than simply a disagreement over strategy. The Sino-Soviet alliance is one of the most important facts of contemporary international life. Communist China constitutes an undeniable factor of physical power on the Communist side of the scales, and her implacable hostility to the United States is an international constant which makes the expansion of her influence fully as dangerous to us as does Soviet expansion. And yet there is also the potential for great trouble between Russia and China in the eventual clash of their rival ambitions and interests. If this potential is fully appreciated and properly exploited, it can benefit the United States in combating their common offensive against the Free World. We must, therefore, concern ourselves not only with their more recent disagreements but with long range considerations as well.

The heart of the argument which has erupted between Russia and China since about 1958 concerns the best way in which to achieve the world victory of Communism. The Chinese disagree with the Soviet decision to renounce the fatal inevitability of war, announced at the 20th Communist Party Congress in 1956, and with the Soviet strategy of "peaceful co-existence" as interpreted by Moscow. China opposes Khrushchev's policy of supporting and encouraging nationalist-minded neutralists such as Nasser, Nehru, Kassim, and Sukarno and, instead, favors support and encouragement for immediate seizures of power by the Communist elements within the neutral countries. The Chinese assert that "imperialism" and, in particular, the United States can be defeated only by war and violence. The Soviets contend that the transition to "socialism" (they say that true Communism has not yet been achieved even in the Soviet Union) can be achieved, generally, by peaceful means without the necessity of international war.

The dispute over strategy, then, stems from the fact that the Chinese are impatient and militant and willing to assume a high degree of risk, whereas the Soviets are convinced that their policy of "peaceful co-existence" is the sure, safe road to victory. The Chinese say Lenin's thesis that imperialism necessarily leads to war and revolution is still valid. Mao Tse-Tung has said that he is willing to accept three hundred million casualties if necessary in order to destroy imperialism by war. Khrushchev insists that basic changes have taken place in the world since Lenin's day and that Lenin himself would have changed his position. The Soviets hurl the charge of "dogmatist" at the Chinese. The Chinese contemptuously retort that the Soviets are "revisionists" and "reformists."

This conflict over policy reached the stage of serious and bitter arguments in 1960. At a meeting of the World "Peace" Council in Rome in January, 1960, the Chinese attacked Khrushchev's policy of seeking to relax tensions with the United States. At another conference in Bucharest, in June of 1960, the issue of limited wars came up. The Chinese insisted that this type of war must be pursued. The Soviets warned that this would involve the unacceptable risk of expansion into general nuclear war. There was apparently a full scale row at that time between the Soviets and Chinese over their conflicting outlooks on the world situation.

The Soviets were clearly disturbed by Chinese militancy. In the summer of 1960, an article appeared in the Soviet press written by Major General N. Talensky which expressed the Soviet viewpoint on war and indirectly challenged the Chinese eagerness to risk it. Talensky said:

As a result of a new global war, the population of the world would be reduced in the final result by half, and at that the most active, capable, and cultured part of mankind would perish. . . . And this would mean that human society would be thrown back and its way to Communism would be immeasurably lengthened.

Then, with obvious relevance to Moscow-Peiping differences, the General went on:

Not to see the danger of rocket-nuclear war is harmful; to see and underestimate it is criminal. . . . Undoubtedly in the event of a new war, capitalism will be finally buried. But is it possible to draw the conclusion from this that sacrifices of war, however heavy they might be, are justified? This would be a harmful, anti-humanist point of view.

And to drive home the point, Talensky added:

It has been shown that limited wars in contemporary conditions will be nothing other than a prelude to a general rocket-nuclear war and one of the forms of unleashing war.[1]

Following this Soviet warning to the Chinese against a too adventurist foreign policy, there was an open presentation of the conflicting Soviet and Chinese theories of revolution. The Soviet viewpoint was expounded in the Soviet Communist Party journal *Kommunist* in September, 1960, to which a rebuttal was made by the Chinese Communist Party organ *Red Flag* in November. In this exchange, *Kommunist* set forth the exact methodology for getting results under the Soviet strategy of "peaceful co-existence." In non-Communist countries, it declared the task must be to strengthen "democracy," that is, the power of the "masses" as against the ruling "monopolists" and "militarists." *Kommunist* gives specific examples of strengthening this "democracy." Among them we can easily recognize some familiar slogans of our day, both in the United States and abroad: there is the "movement for universal peace and against nuclear war"; the "patriotic struggle for safeguarding national sovereignty" (applied, of course, to America's downtrodden friends and allies who have supposedly "sold themselves" to the United States); the struggle "for the defense of democratic freedoms and institutions" (against anyone who is anti-Communist); and the struggle "for the nationalization of the property of the ruling monopolies" (expropriation of the property of domestic and foreign capitalists).

If this program for "democratic revolutions" is followed, said *Kommunist*, Communist parties, at the head of a "democratic" alliance will be able to seize state power without the necessity for a violent revolution. *Kommunist* adds that world imperialism, i.e., the United States, will be prevented from attempting to suppress the revolutionary movements by armed force because the changing world balance of forces allows the Socialist States, with the active support of the "progressive" forces throughout the world, to "paralyze" such intervention. *Kommunist* concedes that "non-peaceful" means of transition to socialism may still be required under certain conditions, but claims that "peaceful revolution is more probable than before for a number of countries and so is the conquest of power without a civil war and an armed uprising."[2]

This brief summary of an important Soviet doctrinal dissertation is presented not only from the standpoint of the argument with the Chinese, but also in order that the reader may perceive that it is a basis for much of Khrushchev's policy toward the neutral and pro-American countries—a policy which was discussed in Chapter III. These statements contain no concept of permanent neutrality for any nation. Neutralism is the perfect climate to facilitate the movement towards a peaceful "conquest of power," which, when the time is ripe, can perhaps take place by means of a relatively bloodless coup rather than by a prolonged armed struggle. It will still be a "conquest" of power, however; and for this to succeed the intervention of the United States must be blocked. This can be done by a combination of the specter of supposed Soviet military power and the "progressive" forces throughout the world including, of course, those within the United States itself. America is to be neutralized from within as well as from without.

The rebuttal in *Red Flag*, which appeared six weeks later in November on the eve of the meeting of World Communist Parties in Moscow took issue with most of the points made by *Kommunist*. The Chinese do not think it will be that easy. According to them, the plan to strengthen "democracy" merely distracted the working class from its "revolutionary prospects," which require that armed uprising and civil war be employed to seize power. Neither the domestic bourgeoisie, said *Red Flag*, nor the imperialist forces—i.e., the United States —will ever reconcile themselves to their doom. They will continue to struggle and to intervene and must be crushed by force.[3]

In this condition of disagreement between the two strongest Communist powers, the meeting of eighty-one

Communist parties took place in Moscow in late November, 1960. All indications point to the fact that there was much heated discussion over the question of peaceful co-existence and the inevitability of war. The Chinese generally stuck to the main arguments that they had put forth earlier in the year. Only the Albanians supported them, however,* and the Manifesto issued at the end of the conference, and to which the Chinese adhered rather than risk an open rupture in their alliance with Moscow, reflects Khrushchev's policies in all of their most important elements. The references to peaceful co-existence, war, and relations with the national bourgeoisie all reflect Soviet thinking. Whatever "compromise" there may have been is alleged to be contained in the reference to the occasional necessity for armed revolutionary struggle, depending on local circumstances. But Khrushchev has always acknowledged this possibility, and "wars of liberation" are an integral part of Soviet doctrine. The Manifesto leaves no doubt that as a matter of practical policy the Soviet and not the Chinese strategy is to be followed.

So much for the overt disagreement on global strategy between Russia and China. The Chinese leaders are no doubt as unrepentant as ever in their views, but they are realists enough to know that they cannot "fight city hall." They seem to have accepted the final draft of the Manifesto with good grace and subsequently there has been

* The somewhat curious alliance between little Albania and the Chinese Communists is based partly on historic Albanian hatred and fear of Yugoslavia, and resentment of what Albania's Communist rulers regard as Khrushchev's "softness" to Tito, compared with the "hardness" under Stalinism.

little outward sign of the squabbling which proceeded the November conference. Soviet handling of the intervention in Laos may well have been dictated by a fear of rash Chinese action, but the two Communist states give every evidence of working in fairly close harmony on this and other international issues.

Over the *short term*—which will cover at least that period required for China to become the equal of Russia in military power—we in the United States will derive little practical benefit from the differences between Russia and China. These will be submerged by their mutual determination to finish us off. Soviet policies will be followed because China lacks the power to follow a unilateral course. The Chinese will probably continue to push for a "hard" line at all times and may be somewhat unhappy whenever Khrushchev employs his tactic of "negotiation." Khrushchev, however, knows what he is doing and is perfectly able to keep his ally in line by the simple device of refusing her promises of military support if she engages in any rash adventures in Asia. He was plainly furious with the Chinese for their incursions into Indian territory along the Tibetan border in 1960, which he considered an unnecessary provocation to India for the sake of worthless bits of territory. China may occasionally resort to such independent actions as this, but there is no indication that she will act in any direct East-West confrontation other than in accordance with the wishes of Moscow.

Actually, the "hard" line favored by the Chinese is very useful to Khrushchev at times. When he wishes to be considered "reasonable," he can point to China and say, "See, I am trying to keep my impetuous colleagues in line. They are constantly pressuring me, and if you do not see things my way, I may have to give in to them, and then there will really be trouble!"

These are all *short term* considerations. Over the *long run*, all the ingredients exist for a death struggle between these two powers. Apart from their common Marxist-Leninist ideology—and it is precisely this that they are arguing about—China and Russia have little in common. Unlike the peoples of the West, the Russians and the Chinese have no similarity of cultural background. The Chinese is perhaps the oldest of man's civilizations, and her ancient emperors considered themselves the rulers of the world long before the inhabitants of the modern Soviet Union had formed even the rudiments of political society. When failure to keep pace with Western military technology exposed China to the depredations of the colonial powers in the nineteenth and early twentieth centuries, Tsarist Russia was among the vultures picking over the Chinese flesh. She obtained railroad rights in Manchuria and the naval base at Port Arthur. In the aftermath of the Bolshevik Revolution in Russia, the Chinese Communist Party was nearly decimated by Chiang Kai-Shek in 1927 because it followed unrealistic advice from Moscow—something which the Chinese have never quite forgiven their Soviet colleagues.[4] Even after the establishment of fraternal bonds of Communist friendship and alliance between the two countries as formalized by treaty in 1950, relations on a government-to-government level have never been particularly cordial. Russia has never "given" China anything. The economic credits and assistance advanced to China by Russia were always the subject of hard bargaining conducted on a purely commercial basis. The Soviets have been plainly irritated by the Chinese effort to skip the socialist phase and proceed directly to Communism, as demonstrated by their establishment of communes—an extreme form of agricultural regimentation which went far beyond the Soviet collective farm. In the summer of 1960, in order to give emphasis to their displeasure with Chinese ideological intransigence, the Soviets pulled nearly all of their technicians out of China on the grounds that they were being "subverted."

More important than either the basic differences or surface frictions are the circumstances of geography and the nature of the phenomenon going on in China. The Chinese population is now in the vicinity of seven hundred million and by the year 2,000 it may well exceed one billion. Such a population, possessed of a fanatical leadership which respects no laws other than the elemental laws of power, and eventually possessing that power in the form of the most modern military weapons, will constitute a threat of the first magnitude to the entire world. But the threat will be most acute to the Soviet Union, which possesses a long common border with China and whose relatively underpopulated Siberian regions offer a tempting target for Chinese expansion.

Khrushchev has frequently snorted at any suggestion that two Communist countries could ever fight each other. In his capacity as a Communist ideologist, it may indeed be difficult for him to believe this, but as a Russian nationalist he is perfectly aware of the dangers to his eastern frontier which great military power combined with the huge Chinese population would present. There is a story, which is quite possibly true, that after the stormy Bucharest Conference, the Chinese sent some military forces across the Soviet frontier and constructed fortifications. These forces were ruthlessly wiped out by Soviet troops. If the Chinese actually did cross Russia's frontier, the action must certainly have given Khrushchev food for thought about the future. Certainly he has avoided giving the Chinese either missiles or nuclear weapons, and he is doing as little as possible to help them in developing a nuclear system of their own—another sore point with the Chinese. Even Soviet assistance to China in building up her conventional military forces seems to have ceased.

The Sino-Soviet alliance is a marriage of convenience founded on the most opportunistic basis. Each needs the other to eliminate their common enemy, the United States. But by now each may be laying plans to destroy the other after that objective has been achieved, or perhaps even in the course of it. At least Khrushchev must by now understand that a Communist World could not be ruled either militarily or ideologically from Moscow without first settling accounts with China. He could very well contemplate turning on China and destroying her with nuclear weapons after the world revolution has been completed. The Chinese, on the other hand, may well have method in their apparent madness for war. They may see in it a means for simultaneously knocking out both Russia and the West and emerging as masters of the world. Ideally, they would like to stay neutral in a nuclear war or at least keep out of the mainstream of nuclear destruction if they could. If not, their cynical attitude is perhaps that enough Chinese would survive to dominate a devastated planet. If, inspite of their protests, Khrushchev's policies are followed and the United States is subjugated without war, the Chinese may calculate that by that time they will be strong enough in their own right to deal with Russia.

Some such ideas as those are very probably going through the minds of the Chinese and Russians at the present time. Their alliance will continue to exist therefore only so long as it continues to be mutually useful. It is obviously much more useful to China than to Russia. Being by far the weaker partner, China has no means for dealing with the United States except with the assistance and support of Russia. If the United States is to be brought to its knees as the first step in eventual Chinese world hegemony, the Soviet Union must be the principal instrument for it. The Chinese are a superpower to be and not a present one. Russia needs China, but she needs her more for psychological reasons than for actual ones. When Khrushchev boasts of the military balance of power shifting to the Socialist states, he is talking almost exclusively in terms of Soviet power. Missiles and nuclear weapons are what counts, he says, and China, so far, has none of these. Khrushchev has seen to that!

As the stronger partner, Russia will control the alliance. As long as it continues to serve her purpose of promoting World Communism *without war,* Russia will maintain it. However, should the Chinese attempt to drag Russia into a war with the United States against her will or should China develop the military strength to act on her own and thus become a serious threat to Russia as well as to the West, the Soviet leaders are likely to conclude that the alliance with China has lost its usefulness to them. That will be the time when they might seek a *genuine* accommodation with the United States as a matter of sheer survival against the Chinese hordes.

Such a Chinese military threat to the Soviet Union is probably still some decades in the future. For at least that length of time, the dominating factor will be their common determination to defeat the United States. It will benefit us little if the eventual Sino-Soviet battle takes place after Western Civilization has been destroyed. If we are to profit from the inevitable clash of interests between the two Communist collossi, we must first defeat their joint effort against us. But the threat which China eventually poses to Russia will, if we take advantage of it, aid us considerably in our own fight for survival.

By taking advantage of it, I certainly do not mean any effort to split the two by diplomatic action such as recognition of Red China, admitting her to the United Nations or abandoning in any way our support of the Nationalists on Formosa. Such a course would not soften Chinese hostility to the United States in the slightest and would only serve to demoralize the anti-Communist forces everywhere. I mean instead that the very fact of China on her border imposes still further limits on Russia's willingness to risk war with the United States—either separately or in support of China—and strengthens our ability to take strong action in a general counteroffensive against Communism with virtually no risk at all to ourselves.

The most disastrous occurrence imaginable for Khrushchev would be a nuclear war with the United States in which the Chinese remained neutral. He knows that if he allowed himself to become involved in war over Berlin or in the course of opposing a United States effort to liberate Eastern Europe the Chinese, contrary assurances notwithstanding, would probably stay out if at all possible. Even if the Chinese were involved, Khrushchev must consider the possibility that the main weight of the United States nuclear arsenal would fall on the Soviet Union rather than on China and that the Chinese would escape relatively unscathed. *Either way, Russia simply cannot afford nuclear war with the United States regardless of how she calculates her chances for victory. If both countries are devastated, the oceans would still protect the United States from physical occupation, but the Chinese could walk into Russia.*

These facts still seem to be generally lost on the American people. I am amazed when some people in the State Department express the conviction that the Soviets would "have" to come to China's assistance if she became involved in war with the United States. This belief betrays, I submit, a profound misunderstanding of the situation. Russia does not "have" to do anything and she would scarcely fight a nuclear war to defend China if a Chinese incursion, say, into Southeast Asia encountered a strong United States military reaction. The Soviets would undoubtedly throw their full weight behind the search for an immediate diplomatic solution if the Chinese got in trouble, but in the last analysis Soviet security is the highest consideration, and the Soviets would sacrifice a potential rival and enemy rather than jeopardize it. We do not need to fear opposing the Chinese because such opposition might involve us in war with Russia.

In a year or two, the Chinese may be able to explode an atomic bomb, although this will not mean an immediate capability to employ it in war. When they do develop their own nuclear weapons in operational quantities, they may well become more aggressive and willing to take risks, but Russia will become even less so, since the Chinese menace to herself will be growing also. The Chinese will still be dependent on Soviet backing for their adventurist policies, and Russia will be even more bitterly opposed to them. If arguments between the two become even more heated and their mutual suspicions increase, the Sino-Soviet alliance could genuinely rupture.

The relationship between China and Russia thus constitutes a great danger to the United States but presents great opportunities as well. We should not take any great comfort from the recent disputes over strategy. These arguments are not likely to undermine the Communist offensive, so long as the tide continues to run so plainly in their favor. The long-term outlook for Sino-Soviet relations, however, is a strong factor in our favor—but only if we survive long enough for the divisive forces in those relations to bear fruit. This requires time, and we do not have that much time unless we can promptly reverse the tide and start winning the Cold War. This, in turn, can be done only by abandoning the defensive.

VI

THE UNITED STATES AND
THE FREE WORLD

A counteroffensive against the forces of World Communism is not only necessary to the survival of Western Civilization, and the United States in particular, but it is certain of success if pushed with vigor, determination, and realism.

The weakness of Communism lies in the fact that it is essentially a tyranny. It cannot be otherwise and survive. Within the areas which they have conquered, the Communists are able to maintain their rule only by various applications of force. In the Soviet Union, to be sure, the regime is attaining a considerable degree of popularity. This is due in part to time, which is eliminating the generation which knew something other than Communism, in part to the relaxation of terror after Stalin's death, in part to the fact that the regime is making genuine efforts to increase consumer production and raise living standards (which an enormous military program would frustrate) and in part to the national pride of the Russian people in the power and prestige of their country. These factors render futile any hope that our problem might be solved by a popular revolution in Russia. Outside the Soviet Union itself, however, these modifying factors are largely or totally lacking. The Chinese Communists are able to divert the attention of their people from serious internal problems only by playing the themes of Chinese nationalism and hatred of the United States. Within the empire dominated by China and Russia, there is at most a sullen acquiescence by the masses of the people. The fallacy of Communism as an ideology is rooted in the fact that it runs counter to man's inherent desires to labor for his own interest, to possess that which he can call his own, to exercise his individuality and to be nationally independent. Communism suppresses one or more of these desires wherever it holds sway. It is therefore a giant with feet of clay. It is an imperialistic tyranny pitted against a free society—a free society, moreover, which continues to enjoy an overwhelming superiority in military and economic power. Once aroused to fight, free men have an inherent advantage over a despotic enemy which only greatly superior brute force can overcome. The problem is that all too often free men do not decide to fight until too late—or that they do not understand how to fight. This has been our particular problem in combating Communism.

By any objective standard of power considerations, the United States should not be in the position that it is in today—retreating before an advancing Communist tide of conquest. We have always been, and still are, *alone* more than a match for the combined Sino-Soviet Bloc. Our people are infinitely more satisfied with our system of government and economics than are the peoples within the Communist World. Communism has nowhere taken power by the ballot, and yet we continue to lose.

In Chapters I and II, I have suggested that we are losing because we have allowed ourselves to be put permanently on the defensive, that we have failed to make effective use of our superior military strength, that we have surrendered too much of our freedom of action to our allies and the United Nations, that we have harbored the illusion that our differences with Communism were negotiable, that we have expected too much from virtue alone, and that we have generally failed fully to fill the role of a great power. We are making these mistakes largely because of certain misconceptions about the world.

I have already described some of those misconceptions about the nature of the enemy. We must now proceed to an analysis of the misconceptions which we continue to hold concerning what we like to refer to as the "Free World"—that great area of allies, neutrals, and semi-enemies, which forms the battleground of the Cold War. Unless or until we decide to carry the war to the Communist World, it will continue to be so. We can neither conduct an adequate defense nor hope to go over to the vitally necessary offense unless we first rectify the mistakes in our thinking about the "Free World." These mistakes are as follows: (1) Europe rather than the "periphery" is our principal concern. (2) The bi-polar world is in the process of breaking down into a plural world of great powers. (3) NATO is, or should be, an alliance among equals. (4) Democracy for all peoples should be our immediate objective. (5) The United States must in all cases respect "world public opinion." (6) The United Nations can serve as a substitute for independent United States action. (7) Neutralism is in the interests of the United States, and (8) Poverty is the principal cause of Communism. We will take these up in turn.

(1) EUROPE VERSUS THE "PERIPHERY." The "Free World" can be broadly divided into six major areas. Four of these are power vacuums and generally underdeveloped. They are tropical Africa, the Middle East (including Islamic North Africa), Southeast Asia, and Latin America. The subcontinent of India, which accounts for almost one fourth of the earth's population, is a fifth region; and lastly there is industrially developed Western Europe, to which Japan can be added qualitatively if not geographically.

The big Communist drive during the decade of the 1960's is being directed toward the power vacuum areas —what President Kennedy correctly called "the southern half of the world." They have already had great successes. If the Communists can obtain at least de facto control over those regions, they will possess the overwhelming majority of the world's population and resources. If they can simultaneously neutralize Western Europe and Japan to the extent that no significant military power center is arrayed against them—and their only real present obstacle in this respect is West Germany—they will *then* be in a position to exert such enormous military and psychological pressure on the United States that we may no longer be willing to run the risks of defending either Western Europe or even our own way of life. The peaceful submission of Western Europe would be little more than a by-product of that of the United States.

India, because of its huge population, exerts an influence much beyond its still rather negligible military power. India is likely to be spared any of the "rough stuff" in the Communist bag of tricks (if the Chinese don't jump the gun) until the very last. Mr. Nehru's tendency to regard Communist intrigues with resigned indifference while displaying great alarm and, at times, indignation over any forceful United States response proves to be very convenient for Khrushchev. If India does not specifically follow the Communist line, its benign neutrality works often enough to the Communist advantage to make its general position a net plus factor in their favor.

When Stalin was still thinking in terms of an eventual war of attrition with the United States, possession of Western Europe, with its great industrial potential, was considered vital to success. This is no longer the case. The Soviets would, of course, like to have possession of all of Europe, but this can be achieved only at the unacceptable risk of using force. The governments and people of Western Europe are too strong and generally too anti-Communist to succumb to any method of indirect conquest. Outright possession of Western Europe is no longer necessary, however, to Khrushchev's strategy. The primary objective of his European policy is to maintain and formalize the status quo. NATO is to be outflanked and allowed to wither on the vine, while the main weight of the Communist offensive surges in another direction.

Khrushchev's principal worry is that a fully rearmed Western Germany would upset the status quo in Europe which he is trying so hard to stabilize. He respects the Germans and their will to fight as he does no other. He may not believe that either France or Britain would fight in a crisis, but he has no doubt about the Germans. Hence his concentration on the German problem, of which Berlin is only a part. All the Soviet proposals on Berlin and Germany as a whole, including those made at the time of the Kennedy-Khrushchev meeting in Vienna, aim at the eventual neutralization of Germany. Any arrangement which would involve the formal or informal recognition of East Germany and the elimination or weakening of the Western position in Berlin would, in Khrushchev's eyes—and probably rightly so—be a big step forward toward a neutral Germany.

There would still be the lesser problem of Western Europe as a forward base for United States military power. To eliminate this annoyance, Khrushchev would be happy to see all Western Europe neutralized. In fact, it is the one area of the "Free World" where he would settle for something like a Western concept of "neutrality." He would gladly abolish the largely fictitious "Warsaw Pact" in exchange for the abolition of NATO. The various plans advanced by some United States intellectuals in favor of "disengagement" in Europe—withdrawal of American forces from Western Europe in exchange for withdrawal of Soviet forces from Eastern Europe is usually the crux of these proposals—might well have been hatched in the Kremlin. We need have no fear that Khrushchev would cheat on such an arrangement. Nothing could please him more.

Barring some such madness by the United States, Khrushchev undoubtedly hopes gradually to frighten Western Europe into neutrality by stressing its vulnerability to nuclear attack. Such neutrality can be brought about psychologically even while the formal alliance remains on paper. Khrushchev even calculates that the major United States allies, Britain and France, will serve as his own allies, in spirit, by pressuring the United States into accepting peaceful co-existence on his terms. The events in Laos serve as one demonstration that he has good reason for such a calculation. And by an ironic twist, the very success of European governments in imposing caution on the United States in the peripheral areas serves to diminish the confidence of European peoples in the willingness of the United States to defend *them* in a showdown. Pacifism increases and a political vicious circle sets in.

We must view Europe in the perspective in which Communist strategy puts it. They no longer consider physical control of Western Europe as vital to victory. Contrary to the stoutly advanced arguments of some commentators, it is not Europe which is of such crucial importance but precisely that "periphery" which they regard with such disdain. It is important to understand that the loss of Laos, Vietnam, Cuba or any other "peripheral" area is a loss of a crucial battle in what is, to the Communists, the *main arena* of combat. We cannot afford any such defeats.

On the other hand, the great importance which Soviet diplomacy attaches to reaching a general accommodation in Europe suggests the obvious: the place where the Soviets are most directly vulnerable to a *counteroffensive* is Germany and Eastern Europe. More on this later.

(2) POWER—A PLURAL WORLD? It is a favorite contention of many who argue in favor of a restrained American foreign policy that the bi-polar world which existed in the immediate post-war years is now in the process of breaking down as more and more nations acquire nuclear know-how and join the nuclear "club." As this process continues, they say, the ability of the United States to exert its influence will steadily decrease. Nuclear weapons will, like the six gun in the Old West, make everybody equal. Something like the old balance of power will be re-established, as nations such as India, Brazil, the United Arab Republic, and even Israel become "great powers." This circumstance will gradually serve to check any further old fashioned Soviet imperialism, and make it not only unnecessary but impossible for the United States to determine the course of events all over the world.

There are a number of flaws in this argument.

It is true, of course, that nearly every nation with access to fissionable materials and some degree of industry can, if it wishes to go to the expense, produce at least an elementary atomic bomb. So far, France has progressed to this stage, the Chinese Communists are undoubtedly close to it, and Israel, with the help of France, has a nuclear reactor, although the Israelis insist it is only for peaceful purposes (the Arabs, of course, are not so sure). But it takes much more to become a great power in the military sense than mere possession of the atomic or hydrogen bombs. This may be of great local importance where there are regional antagonisms, as in the Middle East, but it will not be of great significance on the world scene unless these factors are also present: first, a means of delivery against the prospective enemy; second, a delivery system which is relatively invulnerable to an enemy first strike; third, a territory large enough to avoid total national obliteration in the first stages of nuclear war; and fourth, the national will to use nuclear weapons in support of vital national goals or interests.

Judged against these criteria, the United States and Russia are the only great powers of today and Communist China is the only state apt to become one in the foreseeable future. In the far distant future, India might possess all of the physical qualifications for great power status, but it seems unlikely that the national character of the Indian people would ever lend itself to a huge military establishment, except in the face of a most direct military challenge from Communist China.

China's status as a rival of the United States and Russia in military power is still decades away, but here are all the *potentials* for a real superpower. What the Chinese principally still lack is an industrial base. If they are ever to constitute a direct threat to the United States (or to the Soviet heartland), they must be able to build the long-range missiles which are such an enormous drain on industrial and scientific resources. But, some day, China may be able to do it, for there is no lack of determination—by the Communist rulers, at least.

For at least that period necessary to determine the outcome of the Communist bid to control the world, effective military power will continue to reside with the United States, Russia and to a much lesser, but growing, extent, Communist China. The extreme expense of building a nuclear-missile arsenal, and the futility of it as a means of influencing the fate of the nations whose destinies will be determined by the struggle between the Communist powers and the United States, will work against the rise of any "third force" in the world. If Western Europe were politically unified and possessed of the will to make of itself a great military power center, all of the necessary ingredients are present to become such a "third force." A population of some 328 million, a total gross product of over 300 billion dollars annually and a steel output of 117 million tons a year rank it well ahead of the Soviet Union and in some respects ahead of the United States. Collectively, Western Europe possesses the resources and territorial extent required to become a superpower. But, despite remarkable steps in that direction, complete political unity is still far in the future at best, and the will to make great sacrifices is clearly lacking. The total defense expenditures of the NATO nations plus Spain amount to less than 15 billion dollars annually versus 46 billion for the United States. Defense spending as a percentage of gross national product ranges from 2.8 per cent in Denmark to 7 per cent in Britain, versus 9.3 per cent for the United States.[1] No one European nation—not even a united Germany— possesses by itself the capacity to become a great power in the nuclear age. The European peoples have seen themselves transformed from the actors into the objects of history. They have suffered too much privation in two world wars to willingly undertake the measures necessary to become once more the military masters of their own fate so long as they have a protector in the United States. The years of foot dragging by the NATO nations on their promised military build-up testifies to this. To the extent that West Germany is militarily strong, Western Europe will be an important factor in the military balance of power in the *area of Europe*, but it is unlikely to be a decisive factor in the global balance of power between the United States and the Soviet Union.

(3) NATO—ALLIANCE AMONG EQUALS? The Atlantic Alliance has often been described as the cornerstone or "rock" of American security. From this assumption has flowed one of the most dangerous of the fallacies which has inhibited and circumscribed an effective American foreign policy in dealing with World Communism—the belief that no policy can be pursued which does not enjoy allied unity on at least all major aspects of that policy.

The United States has chosen to treat its two major allies—Britain and France—as co-equal partners in the formulation of global anti-Communist strategy. This means in practice that a coordinated policy can be no stronger than whatever the most timid partner—usually Britain—will support. In the name of an "alliance among equals" we, who alone possess the force to defeat the Communist blueprint for conquest, have surrendered a very great degree of our freedom of action to allies who have lost their capacity to exercise any decisive influence on the scales of history.

This situation came about as a legacy of World War II. Although the war had eclipsed Britain and France as great powers—a process begun by World War I—this fact was not immediately apparent. The most imminent Soviet threat was in Europe; it was predominantly military; and Britain and France, when economically revived and militarily rearmed, were expected to play roles, which if not co-equal, would at least approximate that of the United States in meeting the new threat to world peace and stability which Soviet power and ambitions presented. The same degree of consultation and equality between Britain and America which operated in making the great decisions of World War II was extended to the developing conflict with the Soviet Union. France was likewise accorded her pre-World War II status as a great power. With their colonial empires both nations were still world powers in a military and political sense, and Western strategy came to be a joint affair of the "Big Three."

The tremendous changes in the nature of war which have come to pass in subsequent years, and the dissolution of the British and French empires with the attendant loss of British and French mlitary and political influence have radically altered the situation which prevailed at the time of the formation of the NATO alliance. Where once British and French interests predominated in the Middle East, Southeast Asia, and Africa, there are now only yawning voids filled with turbulent new nations who may, as in the case of the British Commonwealth countries and some of the former French colonies in Africa, retain a certain economic or cultural affinity with their former masters, but whose political destinies no longer depend on decisions made in London or Paris.

The abortive British and French invasion of Suez in 1956 revealed what the nature of the Western World had ceased to be, and what it was becoming in a host of different ways. For the British, Suez was a final attempt to defend a vital British interest by force. For France, it was an effort to exert a decisive effect on the outcome of the Algerian War by eliminating Egyptian President

Nasser, who provided important psychological and military support for the Algerian Nationalists.

The invasion failed, in the first instance, because of the fierce opposition of the United States. We chose to shatter the myth of an alliance among equals not, ironically, over the issue of policy vis-à-vis the Communists, but in defense of the right of small nations to act arbitrarily and illegally against large ones—an action which has haunted us in our difficulties with Castro. Motives aside, however, the United States opposed the actions of its allies. We did not advise or suggest that they withdraw from Suez. We *demanded* it, and we left no doubt that we expected to be obeyed. We spoke with the authority of raw power. In the background was our capability, as a last resort, to employ the Sixth Fleet to compel Britain and France to desist. The second decisive influence working on British Prime Minister Anthony Eden in those dramatic days (it was the British, not the French, who gave in) was the almost solid and extremely vehement opposition of the British Labour Party and the strong opposition of much of the British public. This revealed a state of British public opinion which would have been unheard of in the days of British imperial power.

As a result of Suez, the last pretensions of Britain and France to great-power status were shattered—a circumstance which can be attributed in large measure to United States policy. For France, it marked the turning point in Algeria. From that point on, the French Government lost its will to victory, and the fatal schism which opened between the Army and the Government at the time of the Indo-China defeat in 1954 began to take on major dimensions. This schism was by no means ended when De Gaulle overcame the insurrection of the Algerian generals in April, 1961. For Britain, Suez did more than just ring down the curtain on an imperial era. Since that time, it has been apparent that it would be extremely difficult for any British Government, no matter what its own opinion, to commit Britain to the use of force even in defense against Communism, to say nothing of a counteroffensive against it. This fact has not been lost upon the Communists.

The great lesson of Suez for the United States is the complete European military dependence on us and our own inability to depend on Europe. Despite their justifiable bitterness at our Suez policy, Britain and France did not desert their alliance with the United States. Instead, they have tried to increase their influence within the alliance—to exert through it a power which they do not otherwise possess.

Thus General De Gaulle demands not only that he be consulted on any American action anywhere in the world, but that all decisions be jointly made, that is, that he be given a veto over United States policy. The British insist, in the abstract, that they are willing to fight to preserve the freedom of West Berlin, but they are much more "flexible" than their allies when it comes to defining the point at which a fight must be made. What does Khrushchev think when he sees such a comment as this in the London *Daily Express:* "What do we gain by keeping our troops in Berlin? If the West were to quit Berlin along with the Russians, one danger to world peace would vanish. . . ."[2]

We must understand that NATO is *not* an alliance

135

among equals and will only be an alliance of defeat if we continue to regard it as such. If Khrushchev's problem with his ally, China, is excessive aggressiveness, our problem with our NATO allies is excessive timidity. Their much greater vulnerability to attack makes their outlook inherently different and more cautious than ours. The Sino-Soviet alliance is based on the realities of power. Our NATO alliance is not. We must lead the Western alliance because we are the only nation capable of leading. To put it bluntly, if our allies do not like what we do—and they made it plain that they did not like our efforts to overthrow Castro by force—there is quite literally nothing that they can do about it. If any of them ever go neutral, it will not be because of pique at the United States, but out of fear that United States power is no longer a guarantee of protection.

A policy of victory lies in greater not lesser reliance on our own strength and determination. Western unity is important, of course, but if it is obtainable only at the price of further disastrous concessions to Communism, then we must act as we see fit, let the chips fall where they may.

(4) DEMOCRACY. What exactly do we mean when we say that our goal is to preserve and extend "freedom?" If we mean the national independence of peoples threatened or already held in bondage against their will by the Communists, well and good. This is a realistic and practical objective which we have the power to achieve. If, however, we are still thinking in terms of the Wilsonian slogan of making the world "safe for democracy"—and this is all too often the case—we are impractical, unrealistic and bound to suffer the same disillusion

which was our lot when the post-World-War-I world turned out so differently than the ideal for which we supposedly fought.

One of the greatest mistakes which Americans tend to make is to imagine that the political system which we take for granted and which, together with our system of free enterprise, has made us the greatest nation on earth will work and thrive equally well everywhere else if only people are allowed freely to govern themselves. Applied to many areas of the world, this belief is wholly illusory.

Democracy cannot flourish unless at least two conditions are present: first, a population sufficiently literate and educated to have an understanding of and interest in political issues; and second, love of liberty so great that it will triumph over any temptation to surrender it for the sake of economic or nationalistic expediency.

The most successful experiment in the freedom of the individual as against the omnipotence of the state over a prolonged period of time has been that of the English speaking peoples. That experiment began with the signing of the Magna Carta in 1215. It required almost eight hundred years before anything like a genuine democracy developed in Britain. In the seventeenth and eighteenth centuries, many of those who were dissatisfied with the religious or political persecutions which still prevailed in Britain came to the New World. When the British Colonies won their freedom, the Constitution of the independent United States was drawn up by men who were deeply imbued with the principle of political freedom as a way of life. Even so, the founding fathers were all opposed, in greater or lesser degree, to the unrestricted exercise of the "general will." A government of checks and balances was carefully established, with most of the powers left to the states, in order to protect the rights of the minority against majority rule. Democracy subsequently developed in an environment where there was no history of autocratic rule, where there was little class distinction, where there was a reasonably well educated and informed electorate, and where, up to the present, there were no major foreign threats. This latter condition is particularly important. A people who find themselves beset with serious external enemies or problems sometimes find it expedient to surrender their liberties to the man on horseback. Resentment at the Versailles Treaty plus serious economic difficulties induced the German people to abandon the Weimar Republic and embrace Hitler in 1933. French frustration over the Algerian problem made possible the return to power of General De Gaulle in 1958 and his gradual assumption of dictatorial powers. The United States and Britain are alone among the great powers who have successfully practiced democracy. Others, such as the Scandinavians, adopted it only after passing from the ranks of great powers.

We must come to realize as a matter of practical wisdom that the conditions for the development of democratic government are still partially or totally lacking in that "southern half of the world" which we are now contesting with the Communists. In most of the newly independent nations of Africa, where there is virtually no political sophistication on the part of the populace, democracy in any form remotely similar to our understanding of it cannot possibly work. Nearly every new nation in Africa adopts the forms and trappings of democracy such as a parliament or congress, but the President or Prime Minister soon becomes a dictator in practice if not in name. The Congo is perhaps the most notorious example. The deputies to the Congolese Parliament revealed an almost total ignorance of responsible government and readily sold their allegiance to the highest bidder in the turbulent days after the Congo received its independence.

In the Middle East, religious fervor, tribal loyalties, and the intensely nationalistic emotionalism of many of the people far outweigh any burning desire for democratic institutions. Lebanon perhaps comes closest to a democracy, but the civil war in that country in 1958, stimulated by the intrigues of Egypt's dictator, Nasser, testify to the inherent instability of even this nation.

In Southeast Asia, seventy-five to eighty-five per cent of the people are peasants who have no understanding of, or interest in politics. Among the upper classes, political power is regarded as the means for achieving economic wealth. Power is actually or effectively wielded by the armed forces in most countries, and these people rather than the civilian politicians are the real bulwarks against Communism. The Philippines, long tutored by the United States, is Southeast Asia's only real democracy. There are no other likely candidates.

Even in Latin America where we are most frequently condemned for allegedly backing dictators it is questionable whether the basic conditions necessary for successful democratic governments yet exist in many countries. To the extent that governments are freely elected at all, it is often only with the sufferance of the Army and only with the benevolence of the Army that the President manages to maintain himself against the plots which are constantly hatched to overthrow him.

Ultimately, the conditions necessary for political institutions such as the United States possesses may develop throughout the Free World, but this is a very long range process at best, and it will extend far beyond the probable duration of the Cold War, and then only if the United States wins it. From the standpoint of an historical process, however, it is by no means yet clear that this is the direction in which mankind as a whole is traveling. If the Communists triumph over the entire world, democracy as we understand the term will perish universally. Even if they do not win, the apparent preference of underdeveloped nations for socialistic economies, and the tendency of many capitalist nations to gravitate in the direction of socialism, can lead only to the immediate or gradual ascendency of the state over the individual.

Authoritarian rule is not necessarily tyrannical. The unpopularity of dictatorships often lies more with those who aspire to the power of the dictator themselves than with the broad masses of the people. A government becomes tyrannical when its activities conflict directly and adversely with the interests or aspirations of the masses as a whole, when the individual is drastically limited in his freedom of action, when law and popular consent are suspended, and the secret police become the instrument of coercion. Such is the tragic condition today of Eastern Europe, Cuba, Communist China, North Korea, and North Vietnam. Here the governments have intervened massively in the lives of their peoples in order to bring about social and economic transformations which, accompanied by an extreme police-state terrorism, have proven to be extremely distasteful to broad segments of the population. Here conditions may exist for a general revolt, if the outside assistance necessary to overcome the repressive power of the state is provided.

We must certainly reject that fantastic double standard which says that we should not attempt the overthrow of Fidel Castro in Cuba, whose tyranny has driven thousands into exile and imprisoned tens of thousands more within Cuba, but should reject or abandon authoritarian regimes such as those of Nationalist China, South Korea, or South Vietnam. There is no flow of refugees out of any of these divided nations to join their brethren in the Communist areas. Quite the contrary, the flow of refugees is entirely from the Communist to the non-Communist half. We need only recall the issue of the Chinese prisoners of war in Korea, whose desire to go to Formosa rather than to return to Communist China caused so many difficulties in arriving at a settlement of the Korean War. We should not be blindly against all authoritarian rule but should tailor our policy to each individual situation, keeping in mind the ultimate interests of the United States. The fall of a dictator often opens the way to Communism.

(5) "WORLD OPINION." Some time prior to the ill-fated invasion attempt against the Castro regime in Cuba, I attended a party at which a number of junior Foreign Service officers were present. The question of the United States naval base at Guantanamo, Cuba, and how to defend it came up. There was almost unanimity of opinion by the Foreign Service officers that it probably should not be defended at all, because American defense of

Guantanamo might have an adverse reaction on "world opinion" in general and on that of Latin America in particular. It was suggested that if we were to be asked in the United Nations or perhaps by the Organization of American States (OAS) to surrender Guantanamo to Castro we should do so. It was further suggested that if Castro should send peasants armed with pitchforks against the naval base we could scarcely defend ourselves without being labeled as the murderers of unarmed men, women, and children. The conclusion was advanced that the Guantanamo position was untenable and we had best withdraw from it quietly before we were forced to do so by "world opinion."

The belief that the United States cannot act in defense of its own interests without the sufference of "world opinion" is one of the most dangerous of the current misconceptions on which American policy is based. If we continue to measure the success of American foreign policy by the numbers and intensity of street rioting in Latin America, by hypocritical preachings of neutralist leaders who consider it their right and duty to instruct us in the conduct of our affairs, or by the virulence of the attacks on our policies by pacifist-minded European editorial writers, we will find that the "world" will pat us on the head only so long as we surrender one position after another. We will be truly "liked" only after we are dead.

The United States is the strongest and richest nation in the world. That very circumstance alone inevitably creates a degree of envy and resentment among many of the world's peoples. We are a "have" nation in a world where many countries are "have nots." No matter how much economic aid we may grant to the "have not" countries, the huge contrast in power and wealth will still exist, and we will still be hated for it by some. Among the peoples of Europe, there is still a certain inability fully to reconcile themselves to the sudden eclipse of their nations' positions of leadership. They are unhappy at their secondary position in the world. As their own fears of nuclear destruction—assiduously fed by Soviet propaganda—grow, they tend to blame the United States for the lack of progress towards a genuine peace. They take a certain perverse satisfaction in our discomfiture when our policies go wrong. They question our leadership, and a chorus of criticism sends our "prestige" plummeting. We are distressed. We think it is something that we have done or failed to do. We fail to understand that it is not what we do that makes us unpopular but rather what *we are*.

Following the United States encouraged invasion of Cuba, there were widespread riots against the United States throughout Latin America. Almost simultaneously the United States was approving the first six hundred million dollars for President Kennedy's "Alliance For Progress" program of economic assistance to Latin America. We might ponder the answers to these questions: Was the invasion of Cuba the cause of the riots or was it merely a convenient excuse for the leftists to take to the streets? Suppose we had gone all the way and supported the landings with United States military forces. Suppose Castro had been overthrown. Would the riots have been any worse? Could the Communists have seized power anyplace else in Latin America? Is there any real evidence that any *new* recruits were won to the

Communist cause by the Cuban affair? Will the billions we intend to spend in Latin America really improve our standing with those who riot against us?

India roundly condemned the United States in the United Nations for supporting the Cuban revolution. Outside force, said India, is never justified. This statement came from a nation which absorbed the state of Hyderabad by force and which forceably occupies much of the State of Kashmir today in defiance of the desires of the Moslem majority to unite with Pakistan. Aside from the hypocrisy of the Indian position, one must ask the practical question: Will Mr. Nehru abandon his conception of neutrality and throw his country into the hands of the Communists because he is irritated with the United States?

In Britain the *Manchester Guardian* complained that American policy towards Cuba "has led to a resounding, and deserved, humiliation . . . the Kennedy Administration appears to be guilty of deliberate intervention in the internal affairs of another country."[3] Leaving aside the question of whether Soviet intervention in the internal affairs of various countries *against* the will of their peoples (as in Eastern Europe) justifies in itself United States intervention in support of the efforts of oppressed peoples to throw off Communist tyranny, we might consider also the answers to these questions: Even if such an editorial represented a true consensus of the opinions of the "man in the street"—and this is by no means certain even in Britain—can such opinions be a decisive factor in affecting the outcome of the Communist effort to take over the world? Should we allow Europe to tell us how to act in the Western Hemisphere or any place else where action, if any, will have to be taken by the United States alone?

We cannot expect to be really liked because we are what we are. Only small nations can aspire to popularity. What is important is that we be respected. Respect comes only with power and the willingness to use it. For every person who might have joined the Communist cause in Latin America if we had overthrown Castro, a dozen waverers convinced that we were not going to allow Communism to triumph would have thrown in their lot with us. Our "prestige" throughout the world suffered far less from having planned the operation against Castro than from having bungled it. Worse yet, Khrushchev's warning to President Kennedy that he would render the Cubans "all necessary assistance"[4] left the impression with many Latins that the United States has given up efforts to crush Castro because of fear of Russia. In Southeast Asia, the opposition of the Europeans to intervention in Laos should be weighed against the tendency of the nations of that area to view our actions as a test of our willingness and ability to defend them against the overhanging threat of Communist China.

What, after all, is this world opinion which we worry so much about? Do the mobs which attack our embassies and burn our flags really constitute a good example of "world opinion?" Do the intellectuals and journalists who have sold themselves spiritually or financially to the Communists really represent the peoples in whose name they claim to speak? The truly dangerous anti-Americans are always only a very small minority. The great anti-Communist majority never takes to the streets until they have lost their liberty—and then it is too late, for their protests will be drowned in blood. "World opinion" in many areas is a myth. In most of Africa, it is nothing more or less than the personal opinions of such leaders as Egypt's Nasser, Ghana's Kwame Nkrumah or Guinea's Sekou Touré. Does Nehru really speak for India's 438 million people? Do the votes in the United Nations truly have any relation to the opinions of the peoples supposedly represented? The furious corridor maneuverings and "deals" made on the basis of expediency and arm twisting make it doubtful, to say the least.

If Communism is going to be stopped, the United States will have to do it. No one else can, any more. And we can do it only by proving to those who want to oppose Communism that we will not let them down. It is the good opinion of *these* people that we should seek. When we allowed the people of Hungary to die under the Soviet tanks and abandoned the Cuban revolutionaries to their fate at the Bay of Pigs, we lost prestige where it really counts—among those who are wondering whether to rely on the United States to stop the spread of Communism or whether to make an accommodation with an inevitable wave of history. After Budapest, the people of Eastern Europe decided they had no choice other than to accommodate themselves to a future under Communism. After Laos and Cuba will there not be a tendency among the Asians and Latins to do the same? Not all the propaganda and excuses in the world can overcome the disillusion which is the reward of weakness.

6. THE UNITED NATIONS. If future historians are called upon to write the story of the decline and fall of the United States, the United Nations may occupy a prominent part in the chronicle.

Belgium's Paul-Henri Spaak, the first President of the United Nations' General Assembly, now refers to it bitterly as a "temple of hypocrisy." General De Gaulle asserts that:

The United Nations offers no more than tumultous and scandalous sessions where it is impossible to organize objective debate and which are filled with invectives delivered by the Communists and their allies.[5]

There is much truth in both these statements. The so-called "debates" in the United Nations are seldom more than weary propaganda exercises, in which delegates speak more for home consumption than for the benefit of their listeners and shed crocodile tears to mask the intrigues of their governments.

If the United Nations were no more than a debating society, and if it were guilty of nothing more than the sins attributed to it by Mr. Spaak and General De Gaulle, it would not be the danger to the security of the United States which it is becoming today. Unfortunately, the United Nations has become a major factor in the conduct of the Cold War—a factor which is now tending to work strongly in favor of the Soviet Union.

The United Nations is still regarded by many Americans as the world's best hope for peace. It was so stated by United States delegate Adlai Stevenson in his eloquent statement to the Senate Foreign Relations Committee in connection with his nomination to that position.

The American people overwhelmingly agree that the United Nations is man's best hope for peace. But it is something more than that. It is our best hope for fashioning a peace marked with freedom and justice—a peace which accords with the aspirations of free men everywhere.[6]

Is it really? Have the Communists ever obeyed a United Nations resolution when it did not suit their purpose to do so? Has the United Nations secured the freedom of the people of Hungary or Tibet or any other people enslaved by Communism? Was it a United Nations' resolution or United States troops which stopped the Communists in Korea? (Would there have been even token troop contingents of other United Nations members in Korea, if the Soviet delegate had been present to veto the United Nations resolution authorizing the use of force in Korea? Would there have been any intervention at all?) Was it the United Nations or the blunt warning from the United States which prevented a more active Soviet role in the Congo? In November, 1956, the halls of the United Nations rang with the speeches of United States delegate Henry Cabot Lodge, Jr., who offered the Hungarian patriots indignant oratory instead of the physical help for which they cried so desperately. Said Lodge, five hours after the Soviet attack on Budapest had begun, "if ever there was a time when the action of the United Nations could literally be a matter of life and death for a whole nation, this is that time."[7] Hungary died because the only nation capable of saving it, the United States, chose to let it die—pretending that we could default on our own responsibility by calling upon an organization incapable of handling such a situation. The futility of words when unmatched by action has seldom been demonstrated so tragically as in the case of Hungary. Mr. Lodge's statement stands as its own bitter verdict on the United Nations, and as a warning to others who would put too much faith in it.

The truth is that the issues of war and peace cannot be

decided and the objectives of freedom and justice cannot be achieved by the United Nations. If the world envisioned when the United Nations was established had become a reality—if the Soviet Union had not set out to communize the world, thus precipitating the deadly East-West struggle—the United Nations might have succeeded. But such is not the case. The United States finds itself in a struggle for survival in which the United Nations is slowly being transformed into an instrument for Communist and neutralist attacks on our policies and a straightjacket for our freedom of action. We are becoming increasingly reluctant to take any strong anti-Communist action without the approval of the United Nations. "Let Dag do it," has, as in the case of Hungary and the Congo, become an excuse for United States inaction.

Prior to the tremendous influx of new nations from Asia and Africa, the United States effectively controlled the United Nations. We could always be sure of rounding up the votes for whatever resolutions we proposed. Now all this is changing. The balance of power in the United Nations is held by the Afro-Asian states. Nearly all of them are "neutral," and many of them follow the Communist international line very closely. Almost none see the struggle with Communism as we do. Many hold a double standard in their outlook on the United States and the Soviet Union. At the time of the Cuban invasion we were told by shocked delegates that they expected that sort of thing from Russia but could not understand it from us.

Mr. Stevenson went on to say, in his statement to the Senate, that: "Anyone who doubts the potent if intangible force of the United Nations should consider the eagerness even of Communist regimes to join a club which is, and will continue to be, managed predominantly by its non-Communist members." Managed predominantly by its non-Communist members, *perhaps,* but not any longer by the United States—and therein lies the danger. It is not necessary for the Soviets to control the United Nations, but simply to deny control of it to the United States. The United Nations is no obstacle to the Communist prosecution of "wars of liberation," subversion, and the eventual coups d'état which characterize the strategy of "peaceful co-existence." The United Nations never has and probably never will recognize this as interference in anybody's internal affairs. But, as we have seen, the Communists recognize that these methods will work only if there is no forceable interference from the United States. Here the United Nations can serve as a major Soviet ally by acting as a powerful restraint on United States intervention anywhere. Unless we are willing to act independently of the United Nations, a future action such as the Lebanon intervention may become impossible. It is small wonder that Communist regimes are eager to join the United Nations "club."

The Congo operation is frequently held up as an alleged example of Soviet frustration and defeat in the United Nations. The United Nations and Secretary General Dag Hammarskjold are given credit for keeping the Soviets out of Central Africa. This assertion is considerably wide of the mark. It is quite true that the deposition and eventual assassination of Patrice Lumumba was a severe blow to Soviet hopes to see the entire Congo under pro-Communist leadership. For this setback, Khrushchev blamed Hammarskjold, who was no friend of

Lumumba. Khrushchev's rage, however, is not entirely justified by his fortunes in the Congo. As was pointed out in Chapter III, Lumumba's fall was not the work of the United Nations but of his Congolese opponents; and Hammarskjold's sin, in Khrushchev's eyes, was that he allowed this to happen. The Soviets' new protegé, Antoine Gizenga, has, however, fared very well under the United Nations and almost certainly owes his survival to United Nations benevolence. The United Nations resolution on February 21, 1961, which authorized the United Nations to use force to prevent a civil war, probably saved Gizenga from destruction at the hands of the Kasavubu Government. Should Gizenga somehow buy off or otherwise dispose of his opponents and make himself master of the Congo, the United States will be powerless to stop it. We have completely subordinated our Congolese policy to that of the United Nations, and we cannot determine what that United Nations policy will be.

Khrushchev magnified his fury at Hammarskjold in order to give weight to his demand for a reorganization of the United Nations along the principle of the "troika." He wants the Secretary General to be replaced by three men—representatives from each of the Communist, Western, and neutralist "blocs." Whether or not he will achieve this is still uncertain, but time appears to be on his side. The death of Hammarskjold was a "break" for the Soviets. His successor, U Thant, is only "acting" Secretary General. He was not elected to even this post until the approval of Russia had first been obtained.

The United Nations does serve some useful purposes. It can often control or help to solve minor disputes which are not related to the East-West struggle. And in that struggle, itself, it can serve as a lightning rod and an additional medium of diplomacy against the possibility of war by miscalculation. The United Nations, however, can never solve the Cold War itself. No word said there will ever change the ultimate Soviet objective. On balance, it has now become a positive hindrance to the establishment of that peace marked with freedom and justice of which Mr. Stevenson spoke. Our much heralded "victories" in the United Nations, which consisted in exerting enough pressure to win the votes, will become fewer and fewer. More and more we are being asked to subsidize an organization which will become an instrument of our destruction if we persist in the folly of believing that we must secure its approval of our policies. Above all, the United Nations is *not* a substitute for an independent, strong American foreign policy. It is *not* our best hope for peace unless it be the peace of surrender. Our best hope for a peace with freedom and justice is in ourselves.

(7) NEUTRALISM. Secretary of State John Foster Dulles once described neutralism as immoral. He sought, insofar as possible, to encourage the weaker states along the borders of the Sino-Soviet empire to accept the umbrella of United States military protection and to join in the common cause of repelling the Communist threat to their security, be it external or internal. Dulles has been roundly condemned for this policy by the new philosophers to whom the promotion of neutralism, far from being immoral, should be a positive goal of American foreign policy, at least with respect to the underdeveloped regions. In their view, the "uncommitted" nations

should be encouraged to stay uncommitted. Further yet, where we have commitments to defend weak "client states," we should seek to disentangle ourselves from these commitments.

The role of neutralism in Soviet strategy has been discussed in Chapter III and again in Chapter V in connection with the dispute between China and Russia. To the Soviets neutralism is the half-way point on the road to Communism, for, as Khrushchev says, "All peoples will come to Socialism, to Communism."[8] The trouble, then, with neutralism from a United States point of view is that the concept is not shared by the Soviets. We may choose to abandon our efforts to induce a country to line up with us. The Communists never cease their efforts eventually to subvert the neutral into a Communist state. This is a game which we cannot win. We can only lose.

The apologists for neutralism frequently maintain that the neutrals have no basic affinity for the Soviet system of economics or society, and they are fond of holding up the United Arab Republic and its president, Nasser, as an example of a successful neutralist. The Soviet effort to win him over is regarded as a prime example of a failure of Soviet policy. It is true enough that some of Nasser's actions, notably his crackdown on his own local Communists, have been disappointing to Khrushchev. The Soviets had to swallow hard when Egypt's absorption of Syria in 1958 and the resulting formation of the United Arab Republic broke up a strong Communist position in Syria. Nasser's game of working both the East and West sides of the fence, at which he has become one of the world's great masters, has, of course, produced irritation in Moscow as well as in Western capitals. But it would be premature to conclude from this that the Soviet game is lost in the Middle East. Nasser is a neutralist and an ambitious one. He is ruthless and unprincipled. To realize his ambitions he needs the Soviet Union more than the Soviet Union needs him, because his lust for power cannot be satisfied by legitimate means. Wherever he holds sway, Western influence declines or is eliminated. Nasser seeks to use the Soviet Union for his own purposes when it profits him, and to reject it when it does not. But the sum total of his actions has contributed to a favorable image of the Soviet Union as against that of the West. Russia has become respectable, and the general *climate* for an eventual Communist takeover throughout much of the Middle East has been improved under Nasser's rule. If there is no enthusiasm for Communism as an ideology within the United Arab Republic, neither is there the fierce opposition to it which exists, say, in pro-Western Jordan.

This is the greatest indictment against neutralism. It usually contributes to an intellectual and political atmosphere in which Communism as a conspiracy can thrive. It contributes to complacency and indifference among the people toward that conspiracy. We should never forget the circumstances of the original Bolshevik Revolution in Russia—the most unlikely place of all for a Communist revolution according to Marxist teachings. The October Revolution was carried out by a handful of Communists whose tightly knit organization and tactical planning prevailed against a government which was disorganized, weak, and unsure of itself. Even then, the Bolsheviks initially seized only the capital at St. Petersburg (Leningrad). They subsequently succeeded in gaining control of the whole country not because the Russian people were for them (they were not; the elections to the Constituent Assembly in 1917 left the Communists substantially in the minority, which is why they immediately dissolved the Assembly) but because there was no popular revulsion against them. The Communists won largely by default.

Nasser, at least, does a fairly effective job of controlling his own Communists. Such cannot be said of most of the other neutralist leaders.

In Indonesia, the Communist Party has 1,500,000 members and enjoys substantial representation in the Indonesian Parliament. The Party can scarcely fail to be laying its plans for the day when cooperation with President Sukarno no longer suits its purposes. When the coup d'état comes, will the anti-Communist army be able to stop it? It did so once, when the Communists attempted a rising in 1948, but since then, the armed forces have become heavily dependent on Soviet equipment and training and may well be seriously undermined. Sukarno's long flirtation with the Communists, both internally and externally, has contributed to a state of public opinion which is conducive to a Communist take-over. Indonesia is perhaps the worst example, but we should never forget that there is a Communist Party in nearly every country in the world and that its goal is eventually to seize the government of that country. Regardless of its motives, when a government chooses neutralism, it improves the chances for Communist success.

Neutralism has three main causes, all of which may be factors in some countries. A nation may go neutral because it does not believe the United States is willing or able to protect it against Communist pressures—military or non–military—and seeks to protect itself from such pressure by reaching an accommodation with the Communists. It may believe that there is more to be gained economically by playing both sides of the street—this is the cynical approach which recognizes the Communists for what they are and tries to profit from it—and finally there are those who simply wish to stay out of the Cold War, who view the United States and the Communists in about the same light, and whose nationalistic leaders are extremely sensitive to the charge that they are anybody's satellite. To this latter group belong many of the new African nations.

The United States obviously cannot in all cases prevent neutralism, but we commit a grave error when we persuade ourselves that neutralism can anywhere be in our own interest. What is immoral is not so much neutralism as the eagerness with which the United States now seems to reward it. If we heap more favors on blackmailing neutrals than on loyal allies, we will not long have our remaining allies. If we encourage the naive belief that there can be any such thing as genuine neutrality in the Cold War, we will only promote the success of "peaceful co-existence"—Soviet style—and bring closer the day when Khrushchev's boast of a Communist world will come true. By fooling ourselves, we will find it only that much harder, psychologically, to take the hard steps necessary to defeat Communism. We will find it that much easier, psychologically, to make the deadly compromises which aid the Communist cause. We, at least, should understand the true Communist goal—world domination. We, at least, should understand the role of neutralism in the Communist strategy for achieving that goal. We, at least, should understand that acquiescence in neutralism is incompatible with a strategy aimed at victory over Communism.

(8) COMMUNISM AND POVERTY. In the years 1956 through 1959 a grand total of 27.4 billion dollars in government and private funds flowed from Europe and North America into the underdeveloped nations. Approximately one half of the total and sixty per cent of all government aid came from the United States. Total Soviet aid during that same period was just under 600 million dollars or about one forty-sixth of the total from Western nations. (These figures represent actual disbursements rather than commitments for aid.)[9] It was during this same period that the Soviets began their major effort to penetrate, subvert, and influence these underdeveloped power-vacuum areas. Their success has varied in individual cases but on balance the Communist position in these regions as a whole has steadily strengthened while that of the United States has just as steadily declined. It is time that we started asking ourselves why. The answer lies at least partly in the false assumptions upon which we base our foreign aid.

The greatest myth behind the entire American foreign aid program is the assertion that there is a direct causal relationship between Communism and poverty. The entire propaganda mechanism of the United States Government, from the President on down, is mobilized to impress upon the American people and Congress the thesis that if we can substantially raise the living standards of backward nations, we can also win the battle against Communism in those countries.

157

Such a thesis is based on the assumption, first of all, that the United States has the power to eradicate almost overnight the poverty and want that has plagued most of mankind since the dawn of history. The government is now prepared to admit, as did President Kennedy, that many of the nations that we have been helping are not much nearer sustained economic growth than they were when our aid operation began. It is acknowledged that waste and corruption have plagued our past efforts and that they have been featured by various weaknesses and inadequacies. All this, however, is now to change. Aid is to be appropriated on a long-term rather than a short-term basis. The many agencies responsible for disbursing it are to be consolidated into one. A new emphasis is placed on self-improvement and social justice. Tax reform, land redistribution and sound economic policy are all tied in with the new American foreign aid plans. Frequent parallels are drawn between the United States and the "revolution of rising expectations," alleged to be occurring in Africa, Asia and Latin America. As Secretary of State Rusk put it:

We were once an underdeveloped country ourselves. We grew through a combination of foreign assistance, public aid, and private investment and enterprise. We know that a free society under representative institutions can achieve extraordinary economic growth. . . . Everywhere people are awakening from the stagnation of centuries. They decline any longer to regard poverty and oppression and squalor as the law of nature. They are determined to have for themselves and their children the food they need, housing fit for human habitation, the benefits of their farming, schools, sanitation and medicine, and honest responsible government. They are determined to claim these benefits of modern life without delay.[10]

What the Secretary might have added, but did not, was:

. . . And they expect to have these things, without working for them, as a gift from the United States.

Mr. Rusk's argument is typical of the fallacious reasoning on which so many of the advocates of large-scale economic assistance justify their expectations for success. The comparison is made between the early economic development of the United States—accomplished almost entirely with private capital (much of it foreign, to be sure, but in the form of private investment and not government-to-government grants), under complete political freedom and laissez-faire capitalism, and by an industrious, educated, and extremely aggressive people —and the nations of the southern half of the globe, whose economies are largely socialistic and wasteful, who have frequently exchanged colonialism for dictatorship, and whose people, as in Africa, sometimes assumed that independence meant that they would automatically live in the white man's house, enjoy his way of life and never have to work at all for the rest of their lives. If victory over Communism depends upon giving them what they consider the benefits of modern life "without delay" then our own chances for survival may be rated as zero. But so it is claimed, again and again, as an article of faith. "Foreign aid in the full amounts and with the flexibility requested by the President," declared Rusk, "is vitally—and I mean exactly that—necessary to the continued life of our country and the free world of which it is a part."

Actually, the danger in the present philosophy of foreign aid is not primarily its utopianism which takes a view of the world bearing little relation to reality. The danger lies primarily in the fact that the American people may be lead to misunderstand the true causes of Communism, which are political and psychological rather than economic. The danger lies in the possibility that those who advocate a "soft" policy towards Communism will carry the day arguing that dollars, not bullets, will provide the will to resist Communism—a will which otherwise would not exist. The danger lies in saying, for example, that the "real issue" in the Western Hemisphere is not Sino-Soviet penetration in Cuba but the struggle against poverty in Latin America, and that Castro can safely be allowed to go his way as long as we pull his claws by feeding billions of dollars into the economies of the Latin American countries. It lies in saying that we must pour over 300 million dollars of aid into Laos but should not intervene militarily to defend it against Communist military attack. Referring to his 4.8 billion-dollar aid program "as a vital one in the fight for our own security," President Kennedy said, "I would much rather do it this way than to have to send American boys to do it."[11] The danger lies in this belief that we can substitute money for force in defeating Communism.

Who are the people to whom Communism as an ideology appeals? They are, generally, the politically disaffected, the socially embittered or rejected, the power-hungry opportunists, and the idealists who are unwilling to distinguish the difference between Communist theory and its practical reality. They are students, professors, lawyers, trade unionists, journalists, legislators and, most dangerous, professional revolutionaries who see in the social discontent around them a medium for the violent overthrow of their governments and their own ascension to power. Very few of these people are personally impoverished. The poverty of the peasants may indeed be a factor in attracting the idealists to Communism, but strangely enough the truly poor, the peasants, those to whom President Kennedy referred in his plea for foreign aid as having annual incomes of fifty dollars or less, have never been a good source for Communist recruitment. Even Marx realized this.

The Communists can make no appeal to the peasants as Communists, because Communism runs directly counter to the peasants' individualism. However, by playing on the peasant's fierce longing for land—to him the ultimate source of wealth—the Communists can sometimes win the temporary allegiance of a portion of the peasantry. Hence "land reform" is almost invariably an important element in Communist propaganda. But it is the elemental appeal to the peasant's greed. He is promised that the landowner's property will simply be expropriated and given to him outright, as a gift. Longer range plans such as collectivization are never mentioned. The Communists have no requirement to make good on these promises until after their grip on the country is complete. When that time arrives, they can organize agriculture to suit their purposes with little further regard for the peasants' wishes.

When there is an immediate chance offered him to

seize additional land, as when the Communists manage to start a guerilla movement, a few peasants may be induced voluntarily to fight with the guerillas, but their numbers are never more than a very small proportion of the total. Most of the peasants are at least dimly aware that there is more to Communism than just the seizure of the landlord's land. The great majority remain passive or hostile unless the Communists appear to be winning. In that case, desire for self-preservation can cause a very rapid switch in allegiance.

The enthusiasm for Fidel Castro's revolution among the Cuban peasants was, of course, an important factor in his victory, and the peasants are still an important base for his power in Cuba. However, he won not as a Communist but as a social reformer. Now that he must make good on his promises, his popular support is dwindling, even among some of the peasants. But now he has all of the machinery of a police state to keep himself in power when the unfortunate peasants awaken to their true plight.

Those who maintain that poverty causes Communism should study the facts. The facts do not bear out this contention. In Europe today four of the poorest countries, Turkey, Portugal, Spain, and Ireland have no Communists at all. In Italy, which has a large Communist party, the Communist strength is concentrated in the prosperous industrial north and almost non-existent in the poor, agricultural south. Prior to World War II, the Communist parties were weakest in Eastern Europe— the "poor half" of Europe. Only in prosperous Czechoslovakia were they relatively strong—and then chiefly in the industrialized western area. Despite massive poverty,

Communism is almost non-existent in Pakistan, and weak in India, and Iran, except among westernized intellectuals. There is not, in fact, the slightest evidence that United States aid has decreased the numerical strength of the Communists in a single country.

Those who accept the Communist version of history based on dialectical materialism are not going to be swayed in their economic outlook by any amount of American foreign aid. To these people, Marxism offers the *only* way out of that economic misery which they see about them, and only the destruction of international capitalism as embodied by the United States can lead to the final salvation of mankind. They see our aid merely as a sop to the masses and a cynical effort to promote our own economic imperialism. In short, those who have fully swallowed Communism as an ideology will think no better of us, even if we do achieve a significant boost in the standard of living of backward areas. If we appear to be succeeding, they will only work more furiously against us.

Communism, of course, exploits every popular grievance or aspiration, among which is the desire for economic advance. The Communists, however, flourish and may ultimately triumph because a nation's government is politically or militarily weak and not because its people are economically poor. There may well be a relationship between such weakness and economics, as when nations such as Bolivia or Iran live recklessly beyond their income with resulting inflation and possibly economic collapse. Then there may be great popular discontent against the government and, if the Communists are well organized and alert, an opportunity for a Communist

163

coup d'état. But such a situation is due far more to fiscal irresponsibility, encouraged by the smug conviction that the United States is always there to pick up the tab, than to the basic level of the nation's standard of living.

But what about the Soviet "economic offensive," we are warned! Is this not proof that the Soviets themselves recognize the importance of foreign aid? Well, aside from its minuscule proportions compared to that of the West, we ought to take a very close look at the type of aid the Soviets are extending. There is little attempt on their part to raise anybody's standard of living. Although always billed as aid with no political strings attached, the political motivation stands out like a neon light. In the case of Indonesia, for example, out of a total of about 1.2 billion dollars of Soviet aid *committed* (not disbursed) through early 1961, about sixty per cent was in the form of military equipment. The Soviets already have *sold* (not given) the Indonesians destroyers, submarines and smaller craft, making the Indonesian Navy heavily dependent on the Soviet Union. Crews are trained in Soviet or satellite ports. Medium-range jet bombers, fighters, and army equipment are also flowing into the country. A similar gambit was made in the Soviet arms deal with Egypt, but Nasser's independence has made it much less successful from a political standpoint.

Soviet military "aid" is always extended on a purely commercial basis, and usually on pretty stiff terms at that. It is usually obsolete equipment for which the Soviets have no further need. Economic aid is almost entirely in the form of loans, in nonconvertible rubles. The money must be spent in the Soviet Union. The Soviet "economic offensive" is very small compared to what the United States is doing, and it is always aimed at getting the biggest political splash per ruble. These efforts work well to further Soviet interests, because no effort is made to achieve the impossible. The Russians prefer to let the United States bear the onus when hopes are shattered by reality.

Where the Communists have succeeded, they have succeeded by force; and where they have been beaten, they have been beaten by force. Poverty has not been a factor one way or the other. Nowhere have Communist guerillas ever succeeded in enlisting—other than by various forms of terrorism—the support of the masses of the people. This was true in Greece, Malaya, the Philippines, Burma, Indonesia, and Indo-China—wherever the Communists have tried to seize power by armed action. When they were met by a resolute government prepared to use the necessary degree of counterforce, they have been defeated because they could not win over the people. Where they have had steady access to sanctuary and assistance from across a border, as in China and Indo-China and in Greece—until Tito's defection from the Cominform in 1948 cut off help from Yugoslavia—they have fared much better.

Let the story of the Communist conquest of China be studied well. Mao Tse-tung and his followers survived destruction by Chiang Kai-Shek in the 1930's because they were able to complete the "Long March" to a remote section of northwestern China bordering the frontier of Soviet dominated Mongolia. The Japanese invasion of China in 1937 diverted Chiang's attention to more pressing problems and allowed the Communists to strengthen their position while making only a feeble pretense of fighting the Japanese. After the end of World War II, vast quantities of Japanese arms captured by the Russians in Manchuria were turned over to the Communists, while Chiang's Nationalist armies were delayed or prevented from occupying areas of Manchuria or North China, to their great disadvantage in the renewed civil war with the Communists. Then the United States sought to meddle in the Chinese civil war, arranging truce after truce, always to the benefit of the Communists. As this went on, the Nationalists gradually began to lose hope of victory. A psychological snowball developed which caused the Nationalists to crumble in the space of a few months. The Chinese peasants hastened to get themselves on the winning side. Never was there a better illlustration of the importance of psychology. This is why the Communists work so hard to convince the world that they are the wave of the future. This is why a Soviet victory in the Berlin crisis will have such devastating results.

Communism thrives on weakness. The Communists themselves are superbly organized, disciplined, and determined. This is their great strength. But where they meet an organization, a discipline, and a resolution equal to their own, they cannot possibly prevail. They will always recoil, screaming for "negotiations," hoping that their enemies' resolve will weaken at the conference table and give them an opportunity to win by deception what they are unable to take by force. The answer to Communism, then, is to use our superior strength to keep up a relentless pressure against it. The attempt to raise the standards of living of backward areas should not be confused with the struggle against Communism. Even if we could achieve world-wide social reform and economic advancement, there is not time for these measures to have any decisive effect on the outcome of the great conflict, which is now in its decisive years.

VII

LAOS: CASE HISTORY

On August 9, 1960, a young (twenty-six year old) para-troop captain named Kong Le seized the capital of Laos, Vientiane, with about 750 men and overthrew the pro-American Laotian Government of Premier Tiao Som-sanith. This action set off a chain of events which resulted in one of the most humiliating and possibly far reaching Cold War defeats yet suffered by the United States. In the course of this defeat, the United States displayed almost all of the familiar errors of judgment which we are prone to make about the Communists. We made the mistake of allowing ourselves to be unduly influenced by our major European allies, who are distant from Laos, while ignoring the wishes of our Southeast Asian allies, whose security is directly affected by the events in that area. Worst of all, by our unwillingness to stand fast in Laos, we invited and encouraged World Communism to step up its pressures everywhere else, under condi-tions which seriously undermined the confidence of the non-Communist world in our willingness to resist Communist pressures. Laos is therefore worth examining in detail as an example of how to continue to lose the Cold War.

Captain Kong Le was a neutralist. Although he was trained by the United States, he apparently did not like the fact that the Laotian Government had, since 1958, been strongly pro-American. He blamed the United States for the civil strife going on in Laos between Communist and non-Communist forces and for the corruption rampant among Laotian officials. He claimed that his objective was a genuinely neutral Laos free from outside interference.

It is very likely that Kong Le was encouraged in his actions by the French, who are embittered because of the displacement of their position in Laos by the United States after the Geneva settlement of the Indo-China War in 1954. That agreement, which left Laos independent under a monarchy, provided that the country might receive outside arms up to a level required for self-defense. The French were permitted to retain a small force for training purposes based at Seno in the southern part of the country. However, they had few resources to spare for this purpose, and in the years after 1954, the United States increasingly assumed responsibility for the training of the Laotian Army as well as for its economic support.

The problem in Laos from the beginning was the presence, left over from the Indo-China War, of an armed Communist force known as the Pathet Lao, under the leadership of the "Red" Prince Souphanouvong. They retained control of two provinces, Phong Saly and Sam

Neua, which border on Communist North Vietnam. This gave the Communists a source of outside support. In 1957 an agreement was reached whereby the Pathet Lao leaders were taken into a Laotian coalition government, headed by Prince Souvanna Phouma, half brother of Souphanouvong. A Communist political party was to be recognized; the Royal Laotian Government was to restore its authority in the two Communist controlled provinces; and fifteen hundred men of the Pathet Lao force were to be integrated into the Royal Army.

The Communists used their new position steadily to undermine the royal government. In May, 1958, despite a massive influx of American aid, they succeeded in winning thirteen of twenty-one new seats in elections to the National Assembly. All of the ingredients were present for a Czechoslovak-type coup which would have delivered the country over completely to the Communists. At this point the anti–Communist elements, with United States backing, rallied. In July, the government asked the International Control Commission (ICC), responsible for policing the Indo-China truce, to suspend its operations in Laos; and three days later, Souvanna Phouma's coalition cabinet resigned. A strongly pro-Western regime was then established, and Communist Party leaders were imprisoned. One Pathet Lao battalion fled to North Vietnam while efforts were made, without success, to integrate the outer one into the Royal Army. Later, this battalion escaped from government encirclement and fled into the jungle.

After July, 1958, the United States committed itself to keeping Laos free of Communist control. There were good reasons for this policy.

Laos has, of course, little intrinsic value in itself. Its two million gentle, easy-going, poorly educated people scarcely constitute a nation in the usual sense. They have almost no interest in the outside world or even in their own government and understandably wish only to be left alone, to continue their uncomplicated agrarian existence. But geography and the limitless ambitions of the Communists unfortunately make this impossible. Laos borders on South Vietnam, Thailand, and Cambodia—all targets for eventual Communist domination. Effective control of the territory of Laos will permit the Communists to exert on these countries whatever degree of military or propaganda pressure that may suit their purpose. Strategically, Laotian territory is the expressway for Communist expansion through much of mainland Southeast Asia. It is natural that the Communists should want to control it; vital that the United States should deny them that control.

The charge is frequently heard that John Foster Dulles' policy of maintaining a pro-American Laos was a failure and should never have been attempted. On the contrary, this policy was necessary and generally successful as long as it was pursued with conviction. The great amounts of money spent for economic assistance could not and did not have any significant effect. Most of it dribbled into the hands of grafters. Military assistance and training carried out under the supervision of United States advisors in civilian garb was not an unqualified success either. Nevertheless, the Royal Laotian Army was the only force capable of preventing an internal Communist seizure of Laos, and for two years it did just that—so long as the Communists were afraid to interject any outside assistance. This, in turn, depended on their analysis of United States determination to hold Laos.

That determination was tested, of course. The first probing effort was made in August and September, 1959 (after Dulles was dead). Although press reports exaggerrated the action, Pathet Lao guerillas, operating from bases in adjoining North Vietnam, drove government forces from several positions in the province of Sam Neua. They were aided by North Vietnamese "advisors." On this occasion, swift American reaction, in the form of an alert to the Seventh Fleet, convinced the Communists that the risks of further military aggression were too great. They pulled back. A United Nations fact-finding group, sent in answer to a Laotian appeal, found everything quiet. So matters remained until Kong Le's coup. Thereafter, American firmness wavered, and the Communists acted accordingly.

The first mistake, insofar as the United States is concerned, was our failure to take immediate action against Kong Le. He initially controlled only the capital of Vientiane, and his power rested only on a few hundred paratroopers. His movement did not represent any broad popular upheaval against the United States. The masses of Laotian people were not interested, one way or the other. Furthermore, General Phoumi Nosavan, pro-American Defense Minister in the ousted Somsanith Government, still controlled the bulk of the armed forces, including paratroop elements. He set up headquarters at Savannakhet in southern Laos in opposition to Kong Le. His "uncle" (actually a cousin), the strongly anti-Communist Marshall Sarit of Thailand, backed Phoumi and would have supported him in an immediate attack on Vientiane if he had received any encouragement from the United States. Unfortunately, the initial United States reaction to Kong Le's coup was to "wait and see." The way was thus opened for events to develop into a major crisis and a major defeat for American anti-Communist policy.

Kong Le invited ex-Premier Prince Souvanna Phouma to form a neutralist government in which he, Kong Le, continued to hold the military power. What followed was an exceedingly confused period of political and military maneuvering between the neutralists and anti-Communist elements. During this time, the Communist Pathet Lao re-entered Laos from North Vietnam and began to take control over large portions of the country while the United States was refusing all-out support for either the Souvanna Phouma-Kong Le forces on the one hand or the Phoumi forces on the other. Our initial objective, under prodding from France and Britain, was to persuade General Phoumi to give up his opposition to the neutralists in Vientiane and join Souvanna Phouma's government. We hoped that such a government might contain no Communists. It was clear from our failure to give all-out backing to General Phoumi, the one strongly anti-Communist element, that our policy toward Laos was in the process of changing. We were retreating from a strong position to a weaker one, under the pressure of circumstances and allies, with no clear understanding of what we were doing or where our policy was leading. We were trying to straddle the fence. The ever alert Communists recognized that their opportunity had come.

By the end of October, 1960, the Communist Pathet Lao were in general control of most of the northeastern border areas of Laos and were operating close to Vientiane. They offered their support to Kong Le and his forces who were opposing General Phoumi. Prince Souvanna Phouma, who had practically no control over Kong Le, was gradually being out-maneuvered and driven toward acceptance of the Communists in a coalition government. This in turn hardened General Phoumi against any compromise in his determination to overthrow Souvanna Phouma and Kong Le, and began to convince the United States that a common front against the Communist Pathet Lao would be impossible.

But the United States Government, in October-November of 1960, was in an agony of indecision. On the one hand, there was the faction which favored all-out support for General Phoumi and the restoration of a pro-Western government. This group saw the strategic implications of losing Laos and had no faith in the ability of any neutral or coalition government to avoid infiltration and subversion by the Communists. This view was favored externally by the Philippines and Thailand, both being strongly opposed to any Western retreat in Laos. On the other hand, there was the group which wished to suppress General Phoumi Nosavan and give all-out support to the neutralist regime of Souvanna Phouma. They argued that this was the best that could realistically be hoped for and that the alternative would involve the risk of massive Communist intervention. Britain and France strongly favored this point of view.

On November 10, a pro-Phoumi group seized power in the royal capital at Luang Prabang, leaving the Souvanna government with nothing left but control over the city of Vientiane. Souvanna, who has always had a sincere but naive belief that he could steer Laos on a genuinely neutral course, was now both desperate and angry— desperate because the military situation was going against him and angry because he blamed the United States for undermining him. As usual, United States vacillation and fence straddling was accomplishing nothing and winning us no friends anywhere.

After mid-November, events moved rapidly. The United States, after a final try at promoting a conciliation, decided at last that the victory of Souvanna Phouma would mean an eventual Communist take-over of Laos. He was now completely dependent upon Kong Le and the Pathet Lao to keep himself in power and was agreeing to take the Communists under Prince Souphanouvong, into his Cabinet. He had also established relations with the Soviet Union, which began an airlift of supplies, including military equipment, into Vientiane. The United States still hoped that Souvanna might be induced to resign or forced to do so by a "no-confidence" vote of the Laotian National Assembly. It soon became apparent, however, that a military showdown could not be avoided unless we forced General Phoumi to desist from his plans to attack Kong Le in Vientiane. Despite British and French appeals to the United States to do just that and some further United States hesitation, Phoumi was given sufficient encouragement to carry out a military attack on Vientiane. In the course of a series of coups and countercoups in Vientiane, followed by considerable street fighting between December tenth and fifteenth, Souvanna Phouma fled to neighboring Cambodia, and the Kong Le forces were driven from the capital by General Phoumi, and into the waiting arms of the Pathet Lao, who joined forces with him. The United States now threw its support openly behind Phoumi and the Premier of his new anti-Communist government, Prince Boun Oum.

The stage was now set for the next stage in the Laos drama, and the next serious mistake by the United States. General Phoumi Nosavan had succeeded, despite only luke-warm American support, in driving the neutralists from power. Had he been supported in this objective in August, immediately after Kong Le's coup, the Pathet Lao would not have had the opportunity to extend their control over much of the Laotian countryside, and the problem of Souvanna Phouma and what to do about him might never have arisen. But we still might have forestalled a crisis. Phoumi had the military and—much more important in Laos—the psychological initiative. The United States was generally behind him, and the Royal Laotian Army might well have regained control of the country if we had been willing fully to commit ourselves in support of this objective. It soon became clear that we were not so willing.

As Captain Kong Le and his men, together with the Pathet Lao, retreated northward from Vientiane, the Soviet Union began an airdrop of supplies to these forces as well as to the Pathet Lao base at Samneua, near the border of North Vietnam. According to the American State Department, at least 184 sorties of 11-14 Soviet transport aircraft were carried out between December 15, 1960, and January 2, 1961.[1] This was accompanied by a drumfire of Soviet, Chinese, and North Vietnamese propaganda charging the United States with intervention in support of the "rebel" Phoumi forces against the "lawful" government of Souvanna Phouma. (Souvanna Phouma refused to resign despite his flight to Cambodia.) There were private warnings, notably from North Vietnam, to the effect that she would not "stand idly by" in the face of United States intervention. North Vietnam also called for reactivation of the ICC to police Laos and for a reconvening of the 1954 Geneva Conference. This proposal, endorsed by Communist China, was formally conveyed to Britain by Russia on December 22.

At this point, very strong American action was required, but did not come. The Soviets rather than the Chinese took over the Communist intervention, probably in order to make sure that they could control events. Their airlift, which they never acknowledged and even officially denied to the United States, was a probing action to test our intentions. They knew of the Western split over policy in Laos and obviously hoped that this split would immobilize any strong United States counteraction. They were willing to assume a moderate degree of risk, but they were careful to leave an escape route for a graceful retreat if they were faced with the possibility of a big war. What the United States should have done, therefore, was to have called the Soviet bluff immediately in the form of a private warning to the Soviets that unless their airlift ceased within a certain time period, the United States would shoot down the aircraft. Such an ultimatum would have served notice on Khrushchev that we were quite prepared, if necessary, to go to war to keep Laos out of Communist hands. Unless Khrushchev was prepared to accept the extreme risk of finding himself engaged in a shooting war with the United States—and no United States official believed this to be the case—he would have used his escape hatch, ceased the airlift and contented himself with intensified propaganda attacks. He calculated, of course, that the United States would not resort to such an extreme measure, and his hopes were well justified.

Khrushchev's hopes were well justified because of the unwillingness of United States planners to shape a policy based on their own convictions. Everyone agreed that Khrushchev would not be willing to fight World War III to take Laos away from us. But we were unwilling to say to Khrushchev, in effect: "Look, Laos is as vital to us, strategically, as Berlin is psychologically. We will defend our position there, come what may. If the Chinese or North Vietnamese come in, we are prepared to extend hostilities beyond Laos. This will create the risk of general war, but we are willing to take that risk. Are you?"

Patently, Khrushchev was not, but he was never tested. This was due at least in part to two considerations: We had a poor "legal case." Souvanna Phouma was still recognized as the legal Premier by much of the world. Those who worry constantly about "world opinion" argued that we would be morally isolated if we adopted a very tough policy. Secondly, we would be threatening war against the total opposition of our major European allies. These are the considerations which often emasculate our foreign policy, and they contributed mightily to the disaster in Laos.

United States inaction in the face of Soviet intervention encouraged the Communists to pursue further military action. Aided by at least some units from North

Vietnam, the Communist Pathet Lao struck in force in the last days of December and occupied the strategic "Plaine des Jarres" in North central Laos, with an important airfield at the town of Xiengkhouang. The Soviets poured supplies into this area and soon transformed it into the principal base for further Communist military penetration of Laos. The United States replied with a series of warlike gestures including the dispatch of units of the Seventh Fleet to the South China Sea. The Southeast Asia Treaty Organization (SEATO) met in emergency session on January 2.

Thailand and the Philippines pressed for immediate intervention. Thailand was willing to send her armed forces into Laos if necessary in order to counter intervention from North Vietnam. However, the absolutely implacable opposition of France to any form of SEATO intervention and the almost equally adamant opposition of Britain turned the scales against action and in favor of a "diplomatic solution." Indeed, editorial comment in Western Europe largely condemned even the United States show of force in Laos. By the second week of January, the crisis subsided. SEATO, it was clear, would take no action. The Eisenhower Administration was unwilling to move without the support of our allies, and turned the whole affair over to the incoming President Kennedy. The Soviet airlift went on, unchallenged. Khrushchev had made his move and gotten away with it. The camel's nose was in the tent, and he now became bolder.

At the height of the crisis, on January 1, 1961, Prince Norodom Sihanouk, the now alarmed Premier of neutral Cambodia, proposed a fourteen nation conference to settle the Laos question. Khrushchev promptly supported this proposal on January 2 and continued also to call for reactivation of the International Control Commission. As usual, while there was danger of Western military action, the Communists beat the drums for negotiation, and their military operations quickly fell off to almost nothing. After the failure of SEATO and the United States to take action, however, matters quickly changed. Now it was the West which sought negotiations for the purpose of establishing a "neutral" Laotian government, whereas the Communists suddenly lost interest in such negotiations. Occupation of the Plaine des Jarres left them in an excellent position to consolidate for further military operations. They were still in favor of a conference, of course, but saw no reason why they should not stall as long as possible in order to seize still more of the country and thus improve their bargaining position.

In retrospect, the failure of SEATO or the United States to act in the first week of January, 1961, was probably the fatal turning point in Laos. SEATO was exposed as useless. The French revealed the full extent of their bitterness at the United States for displacing them in Indo-China. The adamant refusal of the otherwise realistic General De Gaulle to sanction any form of intervention cannot be explained on any other basis than "sour grapes"—a still smoldering resentment over American refusal seven years earlier to go to the aid of Dien Bien Phu and a resulting desire to see Laos neutral rather than pro-American.[2] The British were simply acting like the British—professional optimists to whom negotiation is *always* the answer to any East-West problem. Thailand was left especially embittered. The Thais understand full well the danger which a Communist-dominated Laos presents to their security. They are well aware of the end result of a "compromise" solution. When SEATO failed to act, they could not avoid questioning the further usefulness to them of an alliance which was only a "paper tiger" when action became necessary.

The consequences of inaction were most profound on the Royal Laotian Army itself. Although the government of Prince Boun Oum and General Phoumi was legalized by the Laotian National Assembly on January 4, 1961, it was obvious almost immediately that its days were numbered. Prince Souvanna Phouma still refused to resign, and the Communists continued to give him their support. After mid-January, the West was moving toward acceptance of some form of coalition government. The morale of General Phoumi's forces understandably slumped badly. Although never good fighters, they had nevertheless done reasonably well in defeating Kong Le's forces during the battle for Vientiane. When faced by the more aggressive Pathet Lao, they made a much poorer showing. When it became evident that the United States and SEATO were not going to intervene in their behalf and that a compromise was in the cards, it is not surprising that the will to fight on the part of the Royal Laotian Army largely disappeared.

After the Kennedy Administration became responsible for United States policy toward Laos, on January 20, repeated diplomatic efforts were made to persuade the Soviets to cease their airlift and agree to a genuinely neutral Laos, which is what they also professed to desire. The trouble was the definition of "neutrality." The

United States was still foolishly thinking of a Laotian Government without any Communists, whereas the Soviets were now thinking in terms of such a government without any strong anti-Communists. Throughout February, and early March, the Kennedy Administration put out repeated warnings that it would regard Laos as a test of Soviet desires for a thaw in the Cold War. When Ambassador Thompson finally caught up with Khrushchev on March 9, 1961, in the Siberian city of Novosibersk, the Soviet Premier listened politely but made no promises. Meanwhile, the Plaine des Jarres was transformed into a Communist bastion. The Pathet Lao took over the conduct of military operations from Kong Le's increasingly disillusioned neutralists and began to gobble up more and more territory. An effort to set up a three-nation commission of Malaya, Cambodia, and Burma to oversee Laotian neutrality came to nothing. It still did not give the Communists control of the government, and they rejected it. The situation steadily deteriorated as the Royal Laotian Army crumbled.

The most astounding aspect of this period was the apparently genuine but incredibly naive belief of American policy makers that Laos could somehow be kept out of Communist control without the use of force. There is no excuse for such fatuity. The Communists knew they were facing weakness and indecision, and they acted as Communists *always* act under such circumstances: They simply pressed their advantage to the maximum. They ran no risk in doing so. On February 9, 1961, the *New York Times*, which usually reflects administration thinking, made this comment:

There is no disposition in Washington to adopt military measures in support of the Laotian Government. But serious consideration has been given to moves short of that to rally support behind the Boun Oum Government and to end intervention by the Communists through North Vietnam.

We soon found out, of course, that so long as there is "no disposition to use force" there is likewise no disposition on the part of the Communists to cease their own use of force. All of the various United States efforts to temporize and compromise came to nothing.

By mid-March, it was painfully obvious that unless a cease fire were quickly secured, Laos would be lost to Pathet Lao military attack. There would be nothing left to the West to bargain with. Consequently, the Soviets were presented, through the British on March 23, with a demand for an immediate cease fire which would be patrolled by the International Control Commission, consisting of Poland, Canada, and India. If the Soviets would agree, then we would consent to the fourteen nation conference on Laos which they favored. We demanded a quick answer, and we once again brandished the threat of intervention. The marines were alerted, bases were set up in Thailand, and Kennedy made his dramatic televised news conference, in which he said: "If these attacks do not stop, those who support a truly neutral Laos will have to consider their response. . . ."

The President was not entirely bluffing when he uttered those words. The administration was finally aware that we would get nowhere with the Communists unless we were prepared to fight. If the Soviets had ignored the call for a cease fire and if the Pathet Lao had continued their advance—particularly if they threatened to seize either the administrative capital at Vientiane or the royal capital at Luang Prabang—we were prepared to undertake at least limited intervention. Nevertheless, we were still in the process of retreat in Laos. In accepting the Communist call for a fourteen nation conference which would include China and North Vietnam, we agreed, in effect, to hand over the country to the Communists through negotiation. We said we would fight, but only if we were pushed against the wall. We were unwilling to stand by and see Laos conquered by military attack. But we would accept almost anything short of that.

Within a few days, the Soviets and the French arranged to frustrate even this conditional American threat to use force, and thus made it appear that we *were* bluffing. On March 27, Soviet Foreign Minister Gromyko saw President Kennedy and conveyed *in principle* Soviet acceptance of a cease fire. At the same time, SEATO met again in Bangkok to take up the problem. Secretary of State Rusk attended in the hope that SEATO could be persuaded to back up the United States. We were still reluctant to act unilaterally. Thailand, the Philippines, and Pakistan strongly favored intervention. The French, however, declared that they would veto any call to action. The result was a relatively innocuous communique which avoided a specific commitment to do anything. This was not lost on the Communists. On April 2, 1961, Chinese Communist Foreign Minister Chen Yi warned formally that the Chinese would intervene if SEATO did. He said this, of course, only *after* the crisis had passed, and it had become quite clear that SEATO would not intervene.

On April 1, 1961, the Soviets replied formally to the British Note. They blandly agreed to the necessity of a cease fire, but declared that it must be worked out by the Laotians themselves. It was another case of agreeing in principle while stalling in practice. On the same day that the Soviet reply was delivered, a new Pathet Lao offensive began in Laos. The Soviets calculated, correctly, that their acceptance of a cease fire, combined with the inability of SEATO to act over French opposition, would permit them to go on seizing more territory in order to improve their position at the forthcoming conference—which all parties now agreed must be held. With a negotiated settlement always "just around the corner," the United States was under the greatest pressure from Britain and France not to do anything to upset the apple cart. As the weeks dragged on without a formal call for a cease fire, the United States found itself increasingly confounded and frustrated. The Royal Laotian Army continued to suffer defeat after defeat. Once more, in late April, we faced a "moment of truth."

A series of meetings of the National Security Council was held, including a full-dress conference on April 29 at which military and political leaders were present. The Communists countered with the inevitable mixture of threats and conciliation. On April 24, the formal call for a cease fire was issued by Britain and the Soviet Union. The fourteen nation conference on Laos was at last scheduled to begin on May 12; the International Control Commission held its first meeting in New Delhi on

April 28 for the purpose of arranging supervision of a truce. The truce itself seemed all but worked out, and fighting temporarily dwindled. Simultaneously, the Chinese Communists and North Vietnamese hinted that they would intervene if the United States did. In the face of this situation, the United States reached the final decision about May 1 to accept defeat in Laos and fall back to South Vietnam. Those in administration circles who still favored intervention had shrunk to a small minority.

As a consequence of this decision the Geneva Conference on Laos is dragging out its course with weary predictability. The United States is still trying to obtain something short of complete Communist domination of Laos, but the only thing in our favor at the moment is the fact that we still have the *capability* to reverse ourselves and intervene if the Communists push us too hard. Therefore, they seem content to bide their time—consolidating their present military positions while probing to see how far they can go in obtaining control over any new government which emerges from the deliberations. Their minimum objective is military control over enough of the country to allow them access to South Vietnam, Cambodia, and Thailand. Partition might give them this much. Ideally, however, they would like a Laotian government which is ostensibly neutral but which in reality is Communist controlled. This will certainly prove to be the case if Souvanna Phouma is allowed to take over as Premier. The Communists seem destined to achieve their objectives unless the United States reverses its policy. Despite the usual efforts to minimize and conceal the extent of the disaster we have, as things now stand, suffered a profound defeat in Southeast Asia, and our prestige has plunged to an all-time low throughout the Orient.

This defeat need never have happened. It was allowed to happen because of the two great mistakes which we make again and again in dealing with the Soviet Union. We think that to oppose her by force involves the risk of war. It does not on any question not vital to her own national survival. We think that we can achieve an objective by negotiation which we are *unwilling (not unable!)* to achieve by force. This is quite impossible. Khrushchev is well aware of our capabilities. It is our *intentions* that interest him. When he judges that it is our intention to fight, he backs off. When he thinks otherwise, he advances.

The principal argument of the opponents of intervention in Laos centered on the thesis that Laos was not the place for a military showdown with Communism. It would be unwise, they said, to get ourselves bogged down in a possibly endless war in the jungles of Laos. The usual concomitant of this viewpoint was the fear that "escalation," i.e., the progressive increase of forces by each side, could get out of hand and lead to a major war which no one desired. Laos was just not worth such a risk, ran the argument, and anyway, how could we save the Laotians when they were unwilling to save themselves? To Walter Lippmann, writing in late December, 1960, the opposition of Britain, France, and India was the clinching argument against intervention:

What must be avoided, if it is humanly possible to avoid it, is another Spanish Civil War, or another Korea, or another Congo, with the Russians and the Chinese backing one faction and the United States backing another. . . .

The proof that (the Administration) has involved itself more deeply (in the internal affairs of Laos) than was wise is that its policy is under severe criticism in Great Britain, in France, and in India. . . .

. . . Laos is not a primary interest of the United States. For we are not the arbiters of human destiny in every corner of the globe, *and we cannot do more for Laos than India, Britain, and France think it necessary to do.*[6]

None of these arguments for inaction were valid when weighed against the consequences of such a policy. The assertion that the Chinese Communists or North Vietnamese would necessarily have entered Laos in response to United States intervention is particularly questionable. Neither did so, be it remembered, in 1958 when the Communists were thrown out and Laos became a "client" of the United States. The fact of American intervention would in itself serve notice to the Communsts that the United States was resolved to hold Laos. It would then be up to them to weigh the desirability of taking over Laos against the very obvious and very heavy *risk* of doing so by military means against United States opposition. We would have been *committed* and our national and *military* prestige would be irretrievably involved. Laos was in no sense vital even to Soviet prestige, let alone her survival. Khrushchev left himself plenty of escape latches. The Soviets were never prepared to risk a major war over Laos.

As to the Chinese Communists or North Vietnamese, let us concede that their warnings of intervention were

* Italics added.

serious—as were the Chinese warnings about Korea in 1950—even though it must be noted that the two situations were very different. A pro-American Laos is scarcely the military menace to China that a strong army on the Yalu River might have been. If, however, these two states were thinking of intervention, it was probably on the basis of a military action limited to the confines of Laos itself. All the discussion of United States involvement assumed, without question, that we would fight a war strictly *limited to Laos*. This was a serious flaw in our strategy. Why should we agree to fight the enemy's game under unfavorable odds? Suppose we had moved into Laos and at the same time served (privately) solemn notice on Communist China and North Vietnam that any intervention on their part would provoke nuclear strikes by the United States against military targets in North Vietnam and South China. Suppose, in short, that we acted with the voice of raw power over an issue which *we* (not the British or the French or the Indians) determined was vital to our national security. If the Communists still thought we were bluffing and tested us to find out, it might have been necessary to carry out the threat —first by conventional attack, accompanied by an ultimatum to desist immediately, and if that failed, with nuclear weapons. Once the Communists got our message in unmistakable terms *there would be no further intervention*. They would back off because now *they* would be fighting under unfavorable odds. Khrushchev would be no more willing to back China with nuclear weapons than he was in the case of Quemoy in 1958. He wants no part of *international war. Without Soviet support, China cannot risk major military involvement with the United*

States. The Communists would howl and beat their breasts. But we would have control of Laos—and the respect of a reassured Southeast Asia.

Of course, the ambassadors of our European allies would have been constantly at the State Department presenting their protests. No matter! Militarily, we did not need them in Laos. The important thing is that our *Asian* allies would have applauded and supported such a display of American might and determination. In Asia that is what counts. The neutral *leaders,* with Nehru in the vanguard, might well have condemned us, but not with such passion that they would forget to ask us for more money. What does Nehru's rather peculiar psychology count, when weighed against the electric charge of hope which would surge through not only those who wish to avoid Communist domination but those as well who wish to escape from it?

Unfortunately, we did not fight and we will pay a bitter price for our retreat. Just as the surrender of the Sudetenland to Hitler at Munich in 1938 exposed Southeastern Europe to Nazi domination, so does the loss of Laos open the way to a Communist advance in Southeast Asia. South Vietnam is even more vulnerable to Communist infiltration, and shapes up as the next military showdown area. There we may again be faced with the possibility of massive intervention from China or North Vietnam if we do not get out. Thailand, feeling deserted by her SEATO allies, may go neutral. Cambodia can *remain* neutral only by the sufferance of the Communists, a fact not lost on Prince Sihanouk. In Europe the renewal of the Berlin crisis was certainly due at least in part to the disastrous display of Western weakness in Southeast Asia.

Laos again typifies the inability of the United States to deal effectively with the *ambiguous* Communist challenge. We are still thinking in terms of the clear-cut aggression where all the legal and moral considerations are on our side—where everyone in the Free World will get up and cheer us. This is old-fashioned thinking. It won't happen—not in Asia, Berlin, or anywhere else. Some people will attack us no matter how we defend ourselves, or our allies. To the Communists, "wars of liberation" are not aggression, but an overt American response is. Until we realize that this double standard is a fact of life and act anyway, we will keep on losing.

VIII

BLUEPRINT FOR VICTORY

*You may either win your peace or buy it; win it by
resistance to evil; buy it by compromise with evil.*
John Ruskin
The two paths

Conflict has been a constant feature in the development
of human society. From the time that the caveman
crushed his neighbor's skull with a club until the present,
some men have lusted for the possessions of other men
or have sought to exert power over them. Empires and
civilizations have warred against each other in never
ending cycles. Those societies which produced the leaders and citizens equal to the challenges of their time
survived; those which did not, succumbed.

The world of the second half of the Twentieth Century holds no promise that the tendency of man to struggle against his fellow man is diminishing. Our age has
aptly been called the "Century of Conflict." Men still
lust for dominance. Leaders who control nearly one half
the people of the globe proclaim their determination to
inflict their coercive rule on the other half. Within this
giant vortex of conflict, minor struggles constantly erupt
and subside as new political entities arrive on the world

scene and strive against one another for their "place in the sun."

In all of this, power remains the final arbiter in disputes among men. Power takes on many forms, but its basic essence remains military force—the physical means by which one people or society coerces another. Against military force and the willingness to use it, there is only one ultimately effective answer—superior military force and an equal determination to use it. It is futile to talk of the rule of law unless those who uphold it have the power to do so. Law without the means of enforcement is meaningless.

Today, men confront each other not with spears and arrows, but with thermonuclear weapons. This awesome fact does not change the equation of power in the affairs of men; nor does it eliminate man's tendency toward conflict. It may, however, give pause to the modern aggressor *if* he is made to realize that continued aggression involves the clear risk of his own total physical destruction. History is not lacking in examples of peoples willing to perish to the last man in defense of their freedoms. There are no examples of attackers similarly accepting total suicide in order to inflict their will on others; although in the Communist rulers of China there now rises a force which so little values human life that it threatens ominously to do something close to that. If this force thrives, the storm of the present may be but a gentle breeze as compared to the hurricane of the future.

For the moment, however, we, the people of the United States, are confronted by a challenge, World Communism, whose power center is the Soviet Union.

It is this nation which directs the present forces against us. Their goal is nothing less than our total defeat.

The *New York Times,* commenting editorially on the failure of the Western Powers to take retaliatory action after East Germany sealed off the West Berlin border to East German refugees on August 13, 1961, gave one answer to the problem of Communism. Said the *Times:*

> One reason for the hesitant mood is the tragic dilemma facing a democratic society . . . when confronted with an amoral dictatorship pursuing its own advantage under the law of the jungle. While the Soviets seek to stir up revolution and war against us wherever they can—even to the perfidy of the Hitler-Stalin pact—*we must seek to discourage anti-Communist revolts in order to avoid bloodshed and war. We must, under our own principles live with evil** even if by so doing we help to stabilize tottering Communist regimes, as in East Germany, and perhaps even expose citadels of freedom, like West Berlin, to slow death by strangulation.[1]

The section which I have italicized poses, perhaps, the central moral issue of our time: should we abandon those now in captivity and attempt to compromise with evil? I submit that if we accept this philosophy, we are a damned people—damned before God and man. We will have chosen the course of moral and physical cowardice. We will inevitably suffer the just punishment which history relentlessly metes out to the coward.

The *Times* attempted to sweeten the implications of its editorial by continuing with the following bit of soothing nonsense: "History is dotted with the graves of amoral dictatorships while the forces of freedom under

* Italics added.

the moral law march on." History is dotted with the graves of nations and civilizations *period*—moral and amoral. Dictatorships have no monopoly on extinction. There is no divine law in the Universe which says that good shall triumph over evil simply because it is good. If good is to triumph, men must make it prevail. Nazism did not fall because it was evil, but because Neville Chamberlain finally faced his "moment of truth" and resolved to fight. Britain did not accept Hitler's offer of peace in 1939 when the object of her guarantee, Poland, had been overrun by German armies. At last understanding that Hitler's purpose and their own freedom were irreconcilable, the British people fought on to *free* the Polish people. It was a moment of greatness which, for them, seems to have passed.

The great lesson of history is simply that no nation has ever long succeeded in buying off or compromising with an enemy who is not interested in compromise. Khrushchev has forced the choice upon us. We must decisively defeat his challenge if we are going to maintain a world in which we can pursue our legitimate existence as a free and independent people. Victory will not assure a stable world in which there is an absence of human conflict. To believe so would be to disregard all human experience. But failure to defeat the Communist bid for world domination—our *failure to win* will mean the end of any significant United States influence over the future course of world events and the loss of freedom as we now understand the word. We must win in order to survive. The leaders of the Soviet Union are completely ruthless, but all evidence suggests that they are also completely rational. They understand what war would mean to them. It is in the context of this assumption that I suggest a blueprint for victory.

I. WE BEGIN BY INFORMING THE KREMLIN THAT WE INTEND TO WIN. The United States Ambassador to the Soviet Union would be instructed to seek an interview with Nikita Khrushchev in which the Soviet dictator would be informed of the following:

(1) The United States has studied closely Khrushchev's predictions of the ultimate triumph of Communism throughout the world. We take that to mean that in his view permanent co-existence is quite impossible. He apparently has no intention of calling off the Cold War.

(2) We further understand that the method by which Khrushchev proposes to communize us is "peaceful co-existence." We understand him to mean by this that he has set up certain "rules of the game" by which he expects us to abide. These are that we shall not attempt to oppose him anywhere by force nor shall we interfere in any way with those areas already under his control. If we agree to these rules, he promises (for now) that he will not attempt to communize us by means of the overt use of armed force, although he reserves the right to use paramilitary techniques such as guerilla warfare. His rules, of course, deny this right to us.

(3) The United States hereby informs Mr. Khrushchev that it rejects these "rules of the game." We very much regret that he is unwilling to cooperate with us in promoting a genuinely peaceful world. We think that in view of the situation developing on his eastern frontier, it would be very much in the national interest of the Soviet Union to do so. Nevertheless, since it is obvi-

ously his intention to wage relentless war against us and all that we stand for, we now intend to reply by waging war against him and all that he stands for with equal determination. In doing so, we shall fight by our rules and not by his. We do not accept his concept of "peaceful co-existence."

(4) Our objectives do not include the military subjugation of the Soviet Union. They do not include the overthrow of the Communist Party. They do, however, include the liberation of every nation now under Communist control and the destruction of the world-wide Communist conspiracy. We will do everything within our power, short of an attack on Russia itself, to destroy Communism throughout the world and to diminish the influence, power, and prestige of the Soviet Union. We are acting with the legitimate right of self-defense. He has said he will communize us. We do not threaten to capitalize him.

(5) We do not believe Khrushchev's boast that the Soviet Union is militarily equal or superior to us. We regard his unwillingness to couple disarmament with a thorough inspection program to be proof that he is lying about his strength. In any case, we regard the totality of our power—quantitative, qualitative, geographic, and moral—as greatly superior to his. We, therefore, intend to use our superior power in pursuit of our objectives wherever we see fit. We shall not be deterred by threats of retaliation. If he is so foolish as to challenge us militarily, he will be destroyed. We shall maintain the forces necessary to do this. We believe that he has too much common sense to commit national suicide.

(6) As proof that we mean what we say, we shall

henceforth cease all intercourse with the Soviet Union. We will maintain the minimum diplomatic representation necessary to permit a channel of communication, but we will enter into no further negotiations about any subject until we have positive evidence that the Soviet Union is willing to call off the Cold War. The minimum evidence which we will accept in this regard is willingness to withdraw Russian forces from Eastern Europe and to permit genuine self-determination throughout the Soviet colonial empire. Until then, we will cease all economic and cultural relations with Russia. We will do all in our power to persuade or influence our allies to follow suit.

(7) We stand ready to meet Communist force with counterforce at any point and at any level. We will "escalate" our use of force as much as may be necessary to maintain our position, up to and including all-out use of nuclear weapons if no lesser means suffices. We have no interest in compromising with the Soviets on any demands which they may present to us. It is now we who have demands to make upon them. In view of Khrushchev's stated goal of "burying" us, our security demands that those peoples now under Communist control be freed. This is our objective, and realization of it is the price we ask in return for calling off our own "Cold War" against the Soviet Union.

(8) Our efforts to disrupt the Communist Empire will apply especially to Communist China. We regard the unrestricted expansion of Chinese Communist power as the greatest threat now facing the whole of civilization. We are confident that the Soviet Union will someday come to realize that her own interests no less than ours depend

on limiting China's power. In the meantime, we are certain that Khrushchev cannot be so mad as to allow China to drag him into a war against us.

(9) We have no hatred toward the Soviet Union or its people. We regard the promises which Khrushchev makes to his people in the name of Communism as fantasy and we are confident that some day the Soviet people, if given an opportunity, will reject Communism. We make no secret of our dislike of it and all that it stands for. Nevertheless, we are content to co-exist in harmony with the Soviet Union. The measures which we are now planning to take against her are made necessary by Khrushchev's unwillingness to co-exist in harmony with us. Whenever he changes his mind, we will be happy to talk. Wherever the legitimate Soviet security interests can be satisfied without at the same time trampling on the freedoms of other peoples, we will be happy to cooperate. So long, however, as Khrushchev persists in his determination to destroy our way of life, we will give him not a minute's peace. We will wage the Cold War against him with all of our strength.

This declaration should be made in the bluntest possible manner. It should be made public to the world.

Such an interview naturally will not cause Khrushchev immediately to modify his policies. The first reaction would most likely be a red-faced explosion, with the Soviet dictator pounding the table in fury and thundering once more that if we want war we will surely have it—the Soviet Union is the most powerful nation in the world, he would bellow, and the day is long past when we could speak like that, etcetera, etcetera. A tremendous propaganda barrage would follow. Dark threats would issue forth on the pages of *Pravda* and from the microphones of Radio Moscow. The corridors of the United Nations would ring with Soviet declarations that she was being threatened by United States "aggression." Anti-American riots would be whipped up throughout the world with an unparalleled vehemence. Every effort would be made to frighten and then marshall world opinion against the United States. Our nerves and our will would be strained to the breaking point.

The important thing, however, is that the United States cards would be on the table. Khrushchev would be informed of exactly what we intended to do. He would understand the alternatives open to him. Since we would no longer play the game on his terms, he could continue it only at the risk of Russian national suicide. The world would also be informed of United States policy. We would declare, openly and simply, that we are putting our own survival and national interest ahead of all other considerations and that our policies are justified by the inherent right of self-preservation. We would no longer find it necessary to pretend to conform to the cowardly world's double standard of virtue towards an aggressor— the standard which winks at Communist moves but denies us the moral right to defend ourselves. The preservation of our own freedom would depend upon the maintenance and extension of the freedom of others, and we would need no apology and feel no guilt for any action taken toward this end. We would ignore those who screamed that we had no "right" so to act. We would deny their "right" to pass judgment on us. We would put *our* standards ahead of their cowardice, and in so doing save both them and ourselves.

Having made our intentions clear, we should carry them out.

II. WE SHOULD NOT HESITATE TO EMPLOY OUR MILITARY POWER IN LIMITED ACTIONS TO CONTRACT THE BOUNDARIES OF COMMUNISM. At the present moment, especially, it is extremely important to take some piece of real estate away from the Communists. To do so would have psychological consequences of much more importance than the real estate itself. The belief in Communism as the "wave of the future" would be weakened. Soviet inability to prevent us from driving the Communists from power would go a long ways toward exposing her military bluff.

Two areas are immediate choices: Cuba and Albania.

Cuba may not be a "dagger in our heart," but it is far more than a "thorn in our flesh." It is a cancer in the body of Latin America. If not quickly removed, cancer kills the victim. A Communist Latin America would be a very real dagger in our heart. It is indispensible to a successful offensive against Communism that we quickly eliminate it in Cuba.

In order to do this, we should promptly initiate a naval blockade of Cuba and deny her any further Soviet aid, military or economic. Soviet ships attempting to penetrate the blockade would be stopped and sent home. Further efforts would result in their seizure and confiscation. Any attempt by Soviet submarines to stop our ships or interfere with our trade in retaliation would be dealt with by the United States Navy. If this were a cause for war, it would be up to the Soviets to initiate it—and they will not.

Soon after establishment of the blockade, we should once more establish landings on the Cuban coast by

Cuban exiles. This time, however, we should have no hesitation in using United States air power or other support to make sure the landings succeed. A Cuban Revolutionary Government should be promptly established to which we should pledge all necessary help in driving Fidel Castro from power. The Cuban people would then be invited to rise against Castro with this proven assurance that this time *there can be no failure*.

If guerilla warfare is necessary to eliminate the remnants of Castro supporters, we can leave it to the Cubans themselves. The many former Castro guerilla fighters who have deserted him will know how to deal with them. The Cubans will be left free to work out their own political problems in Castro's wake. We will give them what assistance and advice we can, but we will not dictate their choice. The purpose of our intervention will be to enable them to make a free choice. After that we will withdraw.

The liberation of Albania would be a first step in demonstrating to the peoples of Eastern Europe that we intend to act in their behalf and a clear indication to Khrushchev that we intend to create plenty of trouble for him in his own back yard.

Albania is ideally suited for this purpose. It is physically separated from the Soviet bloc by neutral Yugoslavia. Should a revolt break out there, and then be aided by United States military forces, there is no way for the Soviets to interfere short of all-out war. The present state of Soviet-Albanian relations hardly justifies any Soviet risk-taking for Albania in any case. Albania has sided with Communist China in the ideological struggle with Moscow. Eight Soviet submarines, long based at Valona

Bay, Albania, were sent home in June of 1961—
probably an indication of worsening relations.[2] The
Soviets would hardly wish to see Communist rule overthrown in Albania, but there is little that they could or
would do about it.

Communist China can scarcely be considered in the
same terms as Cuba or Albania; nevertheless, attempts
to eliminate Communist rule there should not be wholly
disregarded. If there is anything which can conceivably
be done, it should be tried. The opportunity was missed
in Korea at the cost of possibly fearful consequences to
our children and grandchildren. Although recurrent fam-
ine is a fact of life in China, still the failure of the com-
mune system and the recent food shortages have done
nothing to increase the popularity of the government
with the great masses of the people. No one can say with
certainty that these people would not revolt if given the
chance. They should be given that chance.

Toward this end, we should be willing to unleash and
support Chiang Kai-Shek's army in raids against the Chinese mainland. Our naval and air control over the
Taiwan Straits would enable him to strike anywhere
along a vast stretch of coastline. If this did not bring on
a revolt, it would at least compel the Communists to keep
large numbers of troops spread out over great distances
to guard against attack. The threat of such raids would
create a strategic diversion against any Chinese temptation to send troops into Southeast Asia. To keep Chiang's
army bottled up and immobilized, as we do now, is folly.

In addition to such direct action, it goes without saying that in every case where the Communists threaten
to take an area by force, such as Berlin or Quemoy or

Laos, they should be met with an inflexible determination to resist, regardless of whatever legal pretexts or subterfuges they may employ. We can no longer afford to give up any area of the world without disastrous psychological consequences.

In deterring Communist military attack, it is essential that the United States continue to maintain and improve its capability to fight limited wars. This gives us an all-important alternative to "massive retaliation." A willingness and capability of the United States to fight limited war guarantees that the Communists will meet opposition and the inevitable risk that the conflict will expand into general war—a risk they cannot afford to take.

This risk is credible to them, however, only if we make it plain that we will "escalate" in preference to defeat or prolonged stalemate. There is a great risk in too much emphasis on a willingness to fight limited wars if by this we mean we will necessarily limit ourselves to conventional weapons. It would be foolish to fight in a place like Laos or Quemoy under such limitations. It is essential that we give the Communists to understand that we will use tactical nuclear weapons *if necessary* in fighting limited war. This is particularly important in checking action by the less rational leaders of Communist China, who do not yet have any comparable capability without Soviet assistance. It tremendously enhances the strength of our sea power in operations against land powers advancing against the Eurasian rimlands. It allows the United States to exert military power disproportionate to the resources employed for this purpose. We should not permit any political restraints to be exercised on the possible use of nuclear weapons.

Neither should we entirely discard the *threat* of "massive retaliation." This is still a very plausible threat against Communist China. It is outmoded only in the sense that we should not use it in response to a limited Communist attack when we possess the means to make a lesser response. It is still our ultimate weapon, however, and would lose much of its deterrent value if we said flatly we would never use it except in response to a direct attack on the United States. It is a good principle to keep the Communists guessing.

III. WE SHOULD EMPLOY PARAMILITARY WARFARE AGAINST THE COMMUNISTS ON A LARGE SCALE. Khrushchev's rules of "peaceful co-existence" deny us the right to employ "paramilitary" warfare. This is precisely what we should begin to do openly and on a widespread front.

"Paramilitary" implies any form of operation short of the formal use of regular armed forces. Guerilla warfare, sabotage, terror, subversion, riots, strikes and so on come under this category. It is "dirty" warfare. The Communists are experts at it. We have to learn.[3]

Paramilitary operations must of necessity be conducted in secrecy, but the United States should not hesitate to acknowledge that we deal in such tactics. There is nothing "morally" wrong with a paramilitary offensive against the Communist Empire, any more than it was wrong to wage this type of warfare against Nazi Germany in World War II. The objective in those days was to hasten the defeat of Germany. The objective today is to hasten the defeat of Communism by denying it the sanctuary of a secure base from which to extend its offensive against us. The only real difference is the absence of an all-out shooting war. The ultimate stakes are the same.

Eastern Europe should be made into a principal arena for paramilitary warfare. Having re-established the liberation of Eastern Europe as an objective of our policy, we should immediately encourage *and aid* the people of that area to establish an underground movement and to resist their Communist masters by every means at their disposal. We would tell the satellite peoples: If you want to help us get your own Communists and the Russians off your backs, do everything you can to make it unprofitable for them to stay.

Premature uncoordinated uprisings, which could be crushed by Soviet tanks, would be discouraged, but *preparations* for such uprisings would be carried out, subject to word from us. Sabotage would be conducted against military and industrial targets. The lives of the Communist leaders would be in constant peril. *They* would be the objects of a reign of terror.

The whole of Eastern Europe would be transformed into a net liability to the Soviets—a seething mass of semi-revolt, which would be certain to break into open revolt if a war began. And this nightmare would be made into a constant. The United States would not, as we do now, rule out the strategy of open revolt, nor the possibility of American military support of such a revolt. Our ability to trigger a rebellion at a time and place of our choosing would constitute a powerful club over the Soviets. Like the value of a naval "fleet in being," no matter whether it is actually used, we would have the weapon of a "rebellion in being" to exercise against the Soviets. It would no longer be simply a question of our ability to defend Western Europe with a friendly population. Rather, the Soviets would be forced to consider their own capability to defend a hostile and rebellious Eastern Europe against possible American military intervention.

East Germany, as the most dissatisfied and most geographically accessible satellite, would come in for special attention. We would not do the Soviets the kindness of ruling out intervention by the West German Army in support of a revolt in East Germany, which we might back ourselves, if necessary. The Soviets could not realistically expect much help from the East German Army in such an event; on the contrary, it might join or spark the revolt.

These are the types of things that we can do to make the Soviet position in Eastern Europe untenable. This area is the Soviet Achilles Heel. The aim of Soviet diplomacy is to compel us to recognize the status quo in Eastern Europe. We should *never* agree to this, particularly as it applies to the recognition of East Germany. We should instead give new meaning to our present piously expressed "hope" that these "captive nations" will be freed. We should rekindle the flame extinguished in Budapest and build it into a mighty fire under the feet of the Communist tyrant. We should wipe clean the blot that Hungary put on our own honor and prove that we mean it when we talk of "extending freedom throughout the world."

In Southeast Asia much of the steam could be taken out of the Communist guerrilla operation in South Vietnam if we would begin to wage it in reverse in North Vietnam. We control the sea approaches to this country and the air space over it. There is no reason why we could not enlist and train refugees from North Vietnam as well as personnel from the South Vietnamese armed forces and send them into North Vietnam. As we have found out, a small number of guerrillas can tie up huge numbers of opposing troops. Knowledge that the Communists were getting a taste of their own medicine would certainly encourage resistance to Communist infiltration throughout the rest of Southeast Asia.

IV. THE UNITED STATES SHOULD CEASE IMMEDIATELY TO GIVE NEUTRALISM ITS BLESSING. The Soviet objective of World Communism applies to the neutrals no less than it does to us. If the neutral leaders choose to blind themselves to this reality, there is no need for us to waste our sympathies on them. Where this blindness goes so far that it threatens our security, we have every right to resort to any and all means to change that policy. In some cases this may be no more than a question of a change in leadership.

In many newly independent countries, the strongly anti-Communist elements are not the civilian politicians but rather the military leaders. These men often have a more thorough understanding of what Communism would mean to themselves and to their people than do the civilians—many of whom are heavily indoctrinated with Communist teachings. General Phoumi in Laos, General Nasution in Indonesia, General Ne Win in Burma, and General Mobutu in the Congo are a few examples of this category of individual. They are basically friendly to the United States and its aims. Where we can support them, we should do so. If they feel it necessary to take power, we should aid them—*particularly in those countries whose civilian leaders follow the Com-*

munist line. The pro-Communist "neutral," in other words, is a proper target for United States political warfare aimed at replacing leftist leaders with anti-Communists. If this means a military regime, we should understand that this may be in the best interests of the country and of ourselves.

A military regime is inherently repugnant to most Americans. Nevertheless, where democracy in any case is for the present unworkable, the military regime is often the best path towards democracy's eventual establishment. Less subject to political pressures and corruption, it can serve as a transitional stage until the conditions for democracy more nearly exist. Permanent dictatorship may be less likely to result than under the demagogic politician.

Wherever there is a prospect of a successful revolt by anti-Communists against a leftist government, we should not hesitate to give it our support, including, if necessary, military assistance. One example of an opportunity which was not fully exploited concerns the rebellion which broke out in Indonesia in 1958 against the Sukarno Government. The rebels were protesting in part against the pro-Communist tendencies of President Sukarno. Had it been successful, the danger of a Communist takeover in Indonesia would be much less than it is today.

The reverse of this, of course, is that when a neutralist or pro-Communist coup takes place against a pro-Western government, we should not allow it to stand. Prompt intervention in Iraq in 1958, or in Laos in 1960, would have prevented the loss of these nations to our side.

The argument is immediately raised that we would only be maintaining unpopular American "puppets" in power. To this, I would reply that in the newly independent nations, "popularity" is largely meaningless. Outright or semi-dictatorships exist almost everywhere. Most of the people are politically apathetic. The Communists, who are experts at organizing street mobs, can create a semblance of unpopularity which does not accord with the facts. The supposed "unpopularity" of President Diem of South Vietnam or of the Shah of Iran are cases in point. Let us not be so foolish as to equate popularity with parliamentary democracy.

Where genuine and widespread discontent does exist with the leader of a country over which the United States exerts considerable control—and this was apparently the case with President Syngman Rhee in South Korea, the United States has an obligation to exert its pressure and influence to bring about a change. This should be done, if possible, before a popular explosion brings it about. There are ways to do this.

V. FOREIGN AID HAS A DEFINITE ROLE TO PLAY IN THE COLD WAR—SO LONG AS WE UNDERSTAND ITS LIMITATIONS AND THE LIMITS ON OUR OWN CAPACITY TO EXTEND IT. In Chapter VI, it was suggested that the accomplishments frequently expected of foreign aid are unrealistic; that victory over Communism is not dependent upon the realization of those expectations and in particular upon the eradication of poverty—however desirable that might be; and that a major danger in foreign aid lies in the belief that it can substitute for more vigorous measures in combating World Communism. None of these considerations are in themselves valid arguments for being totally "against" foreign aid, however, if we will first recognize certain facts.

Many of the advocates of almost unlimited foreign aid are fond of pointing out that our present expenditures for this purpose are only an insignificant percentage of our total gross national product and only about ten per cent or so of our annual defense expenditures. These people fail to appreciate the difference between internal and external spending.

The United States can and has engaged in internal deficit financing on a major scale for the past thirty years. Although this has not been without a profound adverse effect on the basic strength of our economy, it has not resulted in an internal economic collapse—not yet anyway. The national debt has climbed to astronomical proportions, but, after all, we "owe it to ourselves" and no man can predict the point at which the camel's back will break.

Deficits cannot with similar indefiniteness be run in an international account. A chronic imbalance in a nation's balance of payments must be corrected or insolvency follows rather quickly. Gold is the international medium of exchange. When there is a net outflow of a nation's gold, it is merely the tangible evidence that the country is spending more than it takes in. Since a nation's gold supply *is* limited (as opposed to a theoretically unlimited national debt), drastic corrective measures are sometimes required. The British Government, as an example, has on more than one occasion been forced to introduce an "austerity" program because of balance of payments problems, most recently in the summer of 1961. These steps were unpopular with the British public, of course. Nevertheless, the British as a whole have enough economic wisdom to realize that they have no choice; opposition is usually over the question of degree rather than the basic program. Unfortunately, no such economic sagacity has yet shown itself in the United States. Since the 1930's, Americans have generally adopted the philosophy that prosperity is their "right," and that it is the proper function of their government to guarantee it to them. The United States Government thereby finds itself imprisoned by the philosophy which it itself promoted. Unwilling to risk expulsion from office by the unpopular step of returning to fiscal sanity, it must run faster and faster to stay in the same place. Economics is a beautifully inexact science. "Experts" profoundly differ with one another. The government can always find and employ those economists who will come up with the necessary theory to support its policies. Thus the fraud of prosperity through deficit financing is perpetuated and the inevitable day of reckoning postponed.

We cannot get away with this policy on an international scale. Foreign creditors cannot be so easily fooled as our own people, no matter how the officials in Washington may try. We have been running a chronic deficit in our international balance of payments, and the chief cause of this is our foreign aid program.

The United States had a favorable dollar *balance of trade* (excess of exports over imports) totaling 4.7 billion in 1960. Of this excess 2.3 billion was financed directly by the government under our foreign aid program and included the export of military equipment. Despite this surplus, total government spending abroad, including 3 billion in military cash outlays (dollars spent by United States military forces overseas) and 3.4 billion in grants and loans to foreign governments, resulted in a basic deficit in our balance of payments of 1.9 billion.[4]

United States Government outlays abroad—military expenditures, economic aid, and loans (net)—have been running between 5 and 6 billion annually during recent years. About half of this amount goes for military expenditures. Under present policies, four fifths of government grants and loans should be spent in the United States, but military expenditures abroad place unrestricted dollars in the hands of foreign recipients.[5] These dollars which are not spent in the United States create the chronic deficit and build up the potential demand which foreigners have on our gold. By the end of 1960, net foreign short-term claims on the United States gold supply totaled about 18 billion or slightly more than the total United States gold stocks.

These demands have not so far been exercised on a larger scale (although we have lost more than 5 billion in gold since 1958) because there has been no compelling reason to do so. So long as the dollar is regarded as sound, there is no reason to convert it into gold. In 1960, however, as it became more and more obvious that our international deficit was becoming chronic, the outflow of gold increased sharply and became front-page news. Foreign speculators, seeing no sign that the United States intended to correct the situation, anticipated a devaluation of the dollar—an increase in the price of gold so as to reduce foreign claims on it—and hastened to increase the outflow of gold through speculative buying. There was an outflow of short-term capital ("hot" money) totaling 1.9 billion, resulting in an over-all balance of payments deficit for 1960 of 3.8 billion.[6] Following emphatic denials in Washington that any devaluation was intended, the gold outflow was temporarily halted in early 1961. An increase in the export surplus in the first half of 1961 to a rate of 6.8 billion, plus some prepayments of money owed to the United States served to hold our international payments in balance for that period.[7]

Such a situation can only be temporary, however, unless the basic cause is corrected. If it is not, the outflow of gold will begin again, and the next time it will be much harder to stop with words. No matter how often it is denied (and governments must of necessity deny any plans to devalue their currency until they actually carry out the step) we will be *compelled* to devalue the dollar if we are unwilling to take other measures to bring our international account into balance. The obviousness of this fact will bring on a new rush of speculation, further stimulate the outflow of gold, and, operating in a vicious circle, hasten the whole process.

What this means is that we must reduce our economic aid if we are to remain financially solvent. We cannot afford even to hold it at its present level unless we can maintain our present export surplus, and this seems unlikely. No permanent improvement in our balance of trade is in sight so long as domestic inflation continues.

It is particularly ironic, in light of the above, that the all-out boosters of foreign aid unthinkingly label as "unthinking" anyone in favor of reducing it. The truth is that we cannot *afford* to be humanitarian on anywhere near the scale that the humanitarians imagine.

All of this being said, we *can afford* foreign aid within reasonable limits. Those totally opposed to it are also mistaken. The criterion for dispensing it is obvious. Expenditures for aid abroad should be reduced to those *clearly and directly* in support of our national objective, which is, or should be, the defeat of World Communism. This means that we must recognize who our friends are and support *them,* rather than our enemies or the neutrals.

The national guilt complex which we seem to feel at being the world's richest nation is mistaken. We prospered primarily because of the industry of our people and the efficiency and stimulus of the free enterprise system. It is not our *duty* to dispense our wealth lavishly and indiscriminately to every nation which lays claim upon it. Ever-growing give-away programs, to any who may ask for them, do not fight Communism—although such measures are always presented to us in those terms. On the contrary, these programs serve only to dissipate the economic strength which is indispensable to a successful offensive against Communism. At present, we are headed down the path to international bankruptcy.

Economic assistance, selectively and intelligently granted to those who believe in giving value for value received can be of great benefit to us and to the free world in the Cold War. This applies particularly to political value. General support for United States policy vis-à-vis World Communism is a legitimate "string" to attach to our aid. Foreign aid should be a weapon of political warfare. It is utterly wasted on those neutrals who blackmail us by threatening to turn to the Soviets if our aid is not forthcoming in ever increasing amounts, and who reward us by spitting in our faces when we ask for their support or understanding.

Pakistan President Mohammed Ayub Khan, on the

occasion of his visit to the United States in July, 1961, delivered an address to Congress which was generally interpreted as a boost to President Kennedy's foreign aid program, then in the throes of the annual Congressional debate. So it was, but Ayub's words scarcely conformed to the philosophy of our foreign aid as at present conceived. It was a plea to the United States to understand who her true friends are and to act accordingly. "As far as the problem of aid is concerned," said Ayub with his characteristic bluntness, "you have to give it to us." But he offers us value in return, and his words ring true:

If there is real trouble, there is no other country in Asia where you will be able to even put your foot in. The only people who will stand by you are the people of Pakistan.

We are pressing against you today as friends, *and if we make good, I think you will in some fashion get it back.** If we don't make good, and if we go under Communism, we then shall still press against you—but not as friends.[8]

This is the statement of a true ally and a valuable friend. Ayub is justifiably angered at an American policy which gives as much or more, proportionately, to neutral India—which is a potential enemy as regards Pakistan—as it does to a loyal ally. "People seem to think that American policy seems to smack of weakness and indecision," Ayub told *New York Times* reporter Paul Grimes after the failure of SEATO to intervene in Laos, which Pakistan was prepared to support with troops.

* Italics added.

It also seems to smack of, shall we say, an inexplicable manner in which friends are considered on the same level as non-friends.

The American policy of encouraging neutrality in areas where we know it will operate in the long run against their interests and their friends' interests is considered incomprehensible.[9]

We should listen to this man, for what he says is common sense. Ayub is a military man himself. The country over which he exerts semi-dictatorial rule has only sixteen per cent literacy, which goes far to explain why such rule is necessary. Yet he is guiding the country on the road to democracy, slowly, by first building it at the local level. We are getting our money's worth in Pakistan, and this country deserves our support. Contrast it with neighboring India, where in 1960 we pledged ourselves to provide over one billion dollars in economic assistance over the following two years.[10] What do we get in return? In terms of political support, almost nothing. As a member of the International Control Commission for Laos, India usually takes the Communist viewpoint and looks the other way as Communist guerillas advance. Nehru attacks our policies at every turn. Perhaps he does so only to appease his Chinese Communist neighbor. Whatever his motives, it does no good to say that he is "honest." The road to the Communist hell is paved with the honest intentions of such as he.

Direct military assistance to countries faced with armed Communist uprisings or guerilla attacks is a wise investment. To the extent that this is in the form of "hardware" provided directly by the United States, it is really an extension of our own defense spending and involves no damage to our international balance of payments.

Economic aid will have to be curtailed and used more as an instrument of Cold War policy. The Soviets know how to do this; it is the reason why they have derived such a high political return on an aid program which is only a small percentage of ours. They cannot really compete with us on equal terms and they do not try. They use aid as an inducement to our allies to choose neutralism (Turkey, Pakistan, Iran, and Thailand have been objects of such offers) and as a reason for the neutrals to stay neutral. *This ugly scheme works only because we let it work.* As it stands today, a neutral may get as much or more aid than an ally.

Let us take the profit out of neutralism. If we are really *for* freedom, then let us cease contributing to the coffers of those governments whose policies support the enemies of freedom. This does not mean that we should require every nation in the Free World to enter into a formal alliance with us. It does mean that nations whose leaders openly sympathize with Marxism and the Soviet Union, praise Fidel Castro, oppose us in the United Nations and otherwise work to frustrate our counteroffensive against Communism shall be given no claim upon us. Let us prove that it "pays off" to be our friend and not our foe.

Let us, especially, cease the absurdity of giving money to Communist governments. In the years immediately after Tito's break with Stalin there was some justification for this in the case of Yugoslavia. Stalin used every means short of war, including heavy economic pressure, to bring down Tito. Tito survived, however, and Yugoslavia has now taken her position as a generally pro-Soviet neutral. She merits nothing further from us. Still less does

Poland. Our purpose should be to free those people from the curse of Communism—not strengthen Communism's grip on them.

These are the methods—military, political, economic, and psychological—which are the prerequisites of victory. They will not appeal to some of our European allies, who will plead for "caution" and "restraint." They will not appeal to many of the members of the United Nations, where their voices will no doubt condemn us. Least of all will they appeal to the free loaders and looters who cry out that their need alone is justification for their demands.

But they *will* appeal to men of courage who are willing to risk their lives to regain their liberty. They will appeal to those staunch and loyal allies who are directly menaced by Communist aggression. They will appeal to those people who understand that there can be no compromise between freedom and tyranny and who are looking for the dynamic leadership necessary to win the fight. And, to put it in the practical terms of international politics, they will appeal to those who want to back a winner.

The Communists have declared war on us; we have not so far declared it equally on them. It is long past the time when we should do so. The United States, in combination with its more determined allies, has the power to compel the Soviet Union to make peace if we will but exercise that power. It will not be easy, of course. We will live in a world of constant crisis, and the danger will seem very great. But the initiative, at last, will be *ours*. The crises will be of *our* making and the dangers will be more to the enemy than to ourselves. *He* will be

219

forced to counter our moves and weigh the risks of action versus inaction. We will press upon him instead of he upon us. When we do this, we will expose the true nature of the enemy. We will find that he is more of a rat than the eight-foot tall monster that we imagine. And, like a rat, he will run.

IX

TOWARDS AN AMERICAN IDEOLOGY

Americanism means the virtues of courage, honor, justice, truth, sincerity and hardihood—the virtues that made America. The things that will destroy America are prosperity–at–any–price, peace–at–any–price, safety–first instead of duty–first, the love of soft living and the get–rich–quick theory of life.

Theodore Roosevelt

Any consideration of the problem of meeting the external challenge to us as a nation inevitably must pose another of scarcely less importance: can we defeat World Communism and still preserve our way of life? There can be no answer to this question unless we can first define what way of life it is that we want to preserve. It is said that we have no American ideology. The charge is true. We have no ideology because we have largely lost faith in the principles which made us a great nation. As a people, we have developed, individually and collectively, an inferiority complex. We are ashamed of ourselves.

We are ashamed to say, for example, that it is free enterprise, the *profit system, capitalism*—not foreign hand-outs—which made us the strongest and wealthiest nation on the earth. We are afraid to point out the blunt truth that wealth cannot be created overnight unless it is to be sweated from the people at the point of a gun. Instead,

221

we are perpetrating on the underdeveloped nations the moral and literal fraud that the Communists are right, the falsehood that there *is* a short cut to prosperity and that Communism's economic successes can be achieved just as fast and quite painlessly by means of massive economic assistance from Uncle Sam.

We assail the teachings of Karl Marx, as expressed in *Das Kapital,* but he seems, nevertheless, to have soiled the word *capitalism* for us. "Capitalist" is a word of opprobrium used almost as much by Americans themselves as by the Communists.

The Constitution established the United States as a federal republic based on a system of free enterprise. On this basis, we prospered and produced the greatest free society the world has ever known. We were fortunate in being granted great natural resources, but other countries have been similarly favored. We succeeded so magnificently because the mainspring of our nation was *individual initiative.* Politically, we did not attempt to impose completely the will of the majority upon the minority. By limiting the powers of the central government, we sought to preserve minority rights. Economically, we provided for equality of opportunity. We put no roadblocks in the way of the man with ability and drive. We knew that our prosperity depended upon such men.

Today, we are in an agony of doubt. We are taught that there are no absolutes, no black and white; everything is relative. It is the era of the worship of security, of mediocrity, of the "Middle of the Road." Unfortunately for us, our enemies have no such philosophy. They believe in the absolute of world domination; of their triumph and our destruction. They believe in black and white.

If we have any "ism" at all in the United States, it might be called "internationalism." This word is respectable; more so, certainly, than old-fashioned "Americanism," which is taken to denote, at best, a narrow-minded provincial outlook out of tune with the modern world. At worst, it is taken to be the slogan of extreme right wing crackpots.

The internationalist type of thinking is in large part responsible for our greatest problem in combating Communism: the loss of the American will to win. Among many advocates of internationalism, there seems to be the feeling that the best hope for peace lies in the possibility that Communism will approach closer and closer to us and that we will approach closer and closer to it until we meet in the middle. These people believe that some sort of world social democracy is the answer to mankind's problems.

A fully socialized economy has never "worked" except by means of force, as is the case within the Communist Empire. There the path has been strewn with the millions of corpses of those who resisted. The advocates of democratic socialism assert that freedom is first of all freedom *from* economic adversity. They forget that there is a higher word than freedom; it is liberty. If economic freedom is to be achieved only by government regulation and paternalism, then this must involve the sacrifice of some degree of liberty. The more socialistic an economy becomes, the larger must be the bureaucracy to manage it. And the larger the bureaucracy, the greater the inherent inefficiency. The rate of growth soon slows down. It can be restored only by concentrating more and more power in the hands of a smaller and smaller group, thus gravitating toward dictatorship. Political liberty, in its highest manifestation, is indissoluble from a free economy.

There are no cases of a completely socialistic democracy. Sweden, which many might cite as an example, is only partly socialistic, with government control over national resources rather than a generally nationalized industry. Even so, the resulting slow down in growth is strikingly evident from these statistics: Between 1950 (the year when West Germany regained its prewar rate of output) and 1955, industrial production gained 79 per cent in free-enterprise West Germany, 41 per cent in Western Europe, but only 15 per cent in Sweden.[1] In Britain an abrupt transition to socialism was attempted under the Labor Government between 1945 and 1951. During this time, the United States provided a total of more than six billion dollars in economic assistance, which was more than the official estimate of Britain's wartime damage. In spite of this, British industrial production in 1951 was only 20 per cent more than the prewar rate compared with gains of 50 per cent for Italy and the Netherlands, whose wartime destruction was roughly comparable.[2] In 1951, the experiment was partially repudiated by the British electorate.

Regardless of whether one agrees with the prescriptions advanced in this book for dealing with the Communist threat, it is an indisputable and unavoidable fact that the United States is a world power, with all that this implies in terms of the "Big Government" necessary to carry out military and foreign policy. A contest with the Communists on any terms must involve this much. Foreign policy and national defense are however clearly the proper functions of government. What is not so clear is whether we can afford to conduct the type of foreign policy necessary to preserve our international security and at the same time engage in the lavish welfare programs that so many Americans have come to expect of their government.

I submit that we cannot. I submit that the continuing effort to "have our cake and eat it too" will not only jeopardize the prospects for ultimate success in the struggle with World Communism but will render any success pyrrhic even if achieved. A people whose plea to their government is "take care of me!" may not possess the necessary fiber to stand up to an external enemy when the chips are down. A people who look to their government to solve their economic difficulties will find that sooner or later they must surrender their liberties as well.

I submit, finally, that an American ideology must be just that—"American." We must first decide what *we* believe in and then make no apologies to anyone for those beliefs. We must rely first and foremost on our own strength and resourcefulness, because we possess them in ample measure. If we believe in freedom, then let us fight for freedom and rally to us all those of like mind. We ourselves possess the greatest accumulation of power the world has ever seen; let us use this power as our own judgment dictates.

To the world, let us say openly, frankly, matter of factly: "We will survive. If you will allow us, we will be your friends. If you will help us, we will do all in our power to help you. But we will not beg your friendship.

Neither will we seek to buy it, which cheapens and degrades you and offers us nothing in return but the scorn and contempt of the blackmailer for the blackmailed. If you side with our enemies, then you will be our enemies also. If we must trample on you to defend ourselves, we will do so.

"If you would be free, then it is in your interest to side with us against tyranny. We have set upon this earth the concept of the freedom of man to develop as he chooses. We will die before we will surrender this right ourselves. But if we must die, then we will die cleanly in battle for our beliefs. We will not die slowly, in degrees, slipping down into the slime of fear, despising ourselves, pretending to be what we are not, trying to conform to your standards of virtue.

"Take us for what we are and know this: With or without your help we will fight and, God willing, we will win!"

NOTES

CHAPTER I

1. *Kommunist* No. 1, January, 1961, quoting from Khrushchev's report, "For New Victories of the World Communist Movement."

CHAPTER II

1. Article I of the Alliance of Friendship and Mutual Assistance between the Soviet Union and the Chinese People's Republic, dated February 14, 1950, reads as follows: "In the event of one of the contracting parties being attacked by Japan or any state allied with it and thus being involved in a state of war, the other contracting party shall immediately render military and other assistance by all means at its disposal."

2. MacArthur, in testimony before the joint Armed Services and Foreign Relations Committee declared that his position, as far as he knew, was practically identical to that of the Joint Chiefs (*Time*, May 14, 1951, p. 21). However, the J.C.S. Chairman, General Omar Bradley, testified that the J.C.S. were opposed to MacArthur's strategy (*Time*, May 28, 1951, p. 23).

3. The original peace feeler in the Korean War was put out by Soviet U.N. Ambassador Jacob Malik in a radio interview in June, 1951 (*Time*, July 2, 1951, p. 21).

4. *MacArthur, 1941-1951*, Charles A. Willoughby and John Chamberlin, McGraw Hill, 1954, pp. 416-417.

5. Speaking in the televised debate with Senator Kennedy on October 21, 1961, Nixon called Kennedy's assertion that the United States ought to encourage an anti-Communist revolt "an

open invitation to Mr. Khrushchev to come in, to come in to Latin America and to engage us in what would be a civil war, and possibly even worse than that."

6. *Goals For Americans,* Prentice Hall, Inc., 1960, pp. 15-19.

7. *Life,* June 6, 1960, p. 110.

8. *New York Times,* December 7, 1960.

9. Philip Mosely, "Soviet Myths and Realities," p. 354, *Foreign Affairs,* April, 1961.

10. *Reader's Digest,* November, 1960, p. 48.

11. Statement made by Dr. Frederick Schwarz, Executive Director, Christian Anti-Communist Crusade, to the staff of the House Un-American Activities Committee, May 29, 1957.

CHAPTER III

1. Stalin, "Sochineniya" (Moscow, Orgis, 1946, VII 13), quoted from Possony, *Century of Conflict,* p. 137.

2. *Nazi-Soviet Relations,* Department of State, 1948, p. 355.

3. "The speech of Comrade G. M. Malenkov at a meeting of the Electors of the Leningrad District of the City of Moscow, March 12, 1954." *Pravda,* March 13, 1954.

4. Khrushchev, speech to the Supreme Soviet, November 6, 1957, *Pravda,* November 7, 1957.

5. *Pravda,* January 15, 1960.

6. *New York Times,* September 9, 1958.

7. S. Titarenko, "Why Wars Are Not Fatalistically Inevitable," *Soviet Russia,* August 17, 1960.

8. *Kommunist,* No. 1, January, 1961, op. cit.

9. *New York Times,* op. cit., December 7, 1960.

10. *New York Times,* November 1, 1961. (Text is as broadcast by Moscow radio, October 31, 1961.)

11. *New York Times,* April 21, 1960.

12. Khrushchev speech August 11, 1961 (*Washington Post,* August 12, 1961).

CHAPTER IV

1. *Pravda,* January 15, 1960.

2. Ibid., October 11, 1957.

3. Ibid., November 29, 1957.

4. Ibid., September 8, 1957.

5. Ibid., November 19, 1957.

6. Ibid., November 18, 1959.
7. *New York Times*, July 9, 1961.
8. *Washington Sunday Star*, December 11, 1960.

CHAPTER V

1. *International Life*, (Mezhdunarodnaya Zhizn) No. 10, 1960.
2. *Kommunist*, No. 13, 1960.
3. *Red Flag*, November 1, 1960.
4. The Soviets urged the Chinese to base their revolution on the urban proletariat rather than the peasantry and to enter into an alliance with Chiang Kai-Shek. Chiang turned on the Communists and almost annihilated them.

CHAPTER VI

1. *U. S. News and World Report*, June 19, 1961, p. 60.
2. *London Daily Express*, June 7, 1961.
3. *Manchester Guardian*, quoted from the *Washington Post*, April 27, 1961.
4. This was the expression used by Khrushchev in his letter to President Kennedy of April 18, 1961. A statement issued by the Soviet Government declared that the U. S. S. R. "reserves the right to take all measures with other countries to render assistance to the Republic of Cuba, if armed interference in the affairs of the Cuban people is not stopped."
5. At a press conference April 11, 1961. See *Washington Post*, April 16, 1961.
6. *New York Times*, January 19, 1961.
7. *Time*, November 12, 1960, p. 31.
8. Khrushchev, speech at meeting of the working people of Moscow, October 20, 1960 (as broadcast by Moscow radio).
9. *New York Times*, March 14, 1961.
10. Testimony by Secretary Rusk before the Senate Foreign Relations Committee, May 31, 1961 (quoted from the *Washington Sunday Star*, June 18, 1961).
11. *Washington Post*, July 11, 1961.

CHAPTER VII

1. *New York Times*, January 4, 1961.
2. Referring to Indo-China during a speech in 1954 De Gaulle

declared: "The United States wishes to hold in check the Soviet bloc but not engage its own troops. They sent money and material to Indo-China but left the French to do the fighting. They are ready to arm any country to fight the Russians and if necessary command their forces for them." *Time*, April 19, 1954, p. 28.

CHAPTER VIII

1. *New York Times*, August 16, 1961.
2. *Washington Evening Star*, June 6, 1961.
3. For an excellent account of the whole paramilitary concept, see the *Wall Street Journal*, May 16, 1961.
4. Figures taken from the First National City Bank monthly letter, July, 1961, p. 80.
5. Ibid.
6. Ibid.
7. Ibid.
8. *Washington Post*, July 13, 1961.
9. Quoted from *Washington Post*, July 9, 1961.
10. *Wall Street Journal*, June 5, 1961.

CHAPTER IX

1. "Twentieth Century Common Sense and the American Crisis of the 1960's," published by the American Institute for Economic Research, p. 44.
2. Ibid., p. 63.